make me
THE BOSS

Mar Chiquita Publishing, LLC
marchiquitapublishing@gmail.com
www.emilytsitrian.com

ISBN: 978-0-578-97183-4 (print)
ISBN: 978-0-578-97258-9 (ebook)

Ordering Information:
Special discounts are available on quantity purchases by corporations, associations, and others.
For details, contact us at www.emilytsitrian.com.

make me
THE BOSS

SURVIVING AS A
MILLENNIAL MANAGER
IN THE CORPORATE WORLD

EMILY TSITRIAN

CONTENTS

chapter 1

A PROMOTION: ONE SMALL STEP FOR MILLENNIALS, ONE GIANT LEAP FOR MEMEKIND

I jumped at the sound of my phone ringing on my bedside table. *Ringing* was a thing that rarely happened to me as a millennial—my friends and I usually communicated over text. As I hesitatingly inclined towards the phone, my chest pounding with fear, I wondered, *Is it a spam call? Liam Neeson, maybe?*

But when I dropped my eyes to look at my phone, I saw my friend's name. *If she's calling, there must be something major to discuss.*

After I picked up and said my confused "Hello?" I got an earful of excited screaming in place of any words. "Okay, what's going on, lady?" I blurted out.

Finally, something comprehensible came out of her mouth: "I GOT PRO-MOTED TO MANAGER!" Even though I may have been left with some minor hearing damage, I was elated for her. She proceeded to tell me I was one of the first people she had called to deliver the news—because I was her friend, but also because of my years of experience coaching first-time managers into this new chapter of their life. The people leaders I've promoted and supported over the years are the proudest legacies in my own career. In many cases, they have even surpassed me in level—some of them have sprung up into impressive Director-level roles and beyond in a variety of industries.

After some emphatic words of congratulations, I told her, by all means, to go out and celebrate, especially since it was Sunday Funday and mimosas exist. After reminding her to stay hydrated, I recommended that she buckle her metaphorical seatbelt for the bumpy but rewarding road ahead: a vague warning.

The line went silent for a moment too long—it was like the excitement was dissipating in real time and being replaced by the all-too-common first-time-manager jitters. This also happens to be the exact reason why I told her to, in simpler terms, get in that mimosa now.

"What do you mean?" she asked. "What 'bumpy road'?"

I knew she wasn't expecting her new position to be easy. Instead, she was realizing how much she didn't know yet. So, I laid out an extensive guide—the "inside baseball," if you will.

My friend, like so many of you reading, wanted to be the best people manager possible, especially since she had had some less-than-good experiences with bosses (haven't we all?).

After finishing my monologue, I heard a sigh of relief on the other end of the line as she thanked me. But there was one question I couldn't answer.

"Do you recommend any books to help me get going?"

"Uhh—" I murmured, then froze.

I mentally filed through the countless business and leadership books I had once read and studied when I was in my friend's situation years ago, right after the startup I had joined got their Series A funding and went on a hiring spree. By default, we early employees became heads of department overnight and were instructed to start building our teams immediately.

I remember asking my boss at the time how to build out a department like the one I had taken on.

"Ummm, I'm not sure—go to some conferences? Read some books? Figure it out!"

And so, of course I did. I downloaded as many audiobooks as my iPhone 5 could handle, and devoured the content every free moment I could find. Did they help?

Most of the books helped me to *some* extent, but turned out to be overwhelmingly lackluster and dated. The working world looks a lot different today, noticeably less male, more diverse, and with a different set of priorities. Few of them addressed the elephant in the room—how the hell a 20-something employee with just a few years' work experience is supposed to figure out how to become a people manager at a tech company in hypergrowth mode overnight.

Most importantly, they failed to address the complexities of people management in the modern business era, especially as a younger manager coming up in a technology-saturated world peppered with generation-defining #MeToo, #BlackLivesMatter, and other social movements.

In my moment of reflection, I realized that my friend was probably one of thousands, if not millions, of first-time, millennial people managers that could use some extra help navigating the new business climate as well as their newfound power.

And that's when this book was born.

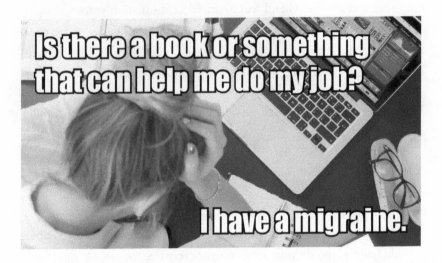

Let's face it: The business world has changed, big-time. The average age of a first-time manager is 30, smack-dab in the middle of the millennial generation (1981–1996). Yes, the decade-plus that produced modern wonders, such as Nirvana, the fall of the Berlin Wall, and the musical *Rent* also produced 75 million of us avocado toast–obsessed millennials. In fact, the Department of Labor estimates between five and 11 million of us are now in management jobs.[1]

Love us or hate us, we're here and we're taking the lead. So, let's take the lead!

This guide was made to help people like you and the millions of other novice business managers adjust to this new, fabulous, terrifying, and hilarious next chapter, while becoming the boss you've always wanted to work for.

In this book, you will learn some of the basic tactical guidance you'll need to #BossUp, such as how to do the following:

---

1   Chris Taylor, "The Millennial Managers Have Arrived," Miles Lehane, August 5, 2019, https://www.mileslehane.com/blog/the-millennial-managers-have-arrived.

- Deal with expenses like a pro

- Manage paid time off (PTO) and other leave...without making anyone cry

- Do the Big H (Hiring)

- Handle escalations (Wheee!)

- Give an A++ performance review

- Not screw up your career by focusing on the wrong things (NSUYCFWT)

But, as the saying goes, "Man cannot live on bread alone," which really should be followed by, "bosses of all genders cannot thrive on expense reports alone."

Let's be real: Your life and career have both shifted in a monumental way. If you're anything like the millions of fellow millennials taking on people management for the first time, you didn't take the job just for the thrill of approving a cell phone reimbursement.

You're here to make a difference, aren't you? To blaze a trail in the big world of business. To align your career with your core values. To do work you know you'll be proud of years down the line.

The truth is, you can't do all of that in your new position without learning the soft skills required to succeed. Therefore, in addition to the practical advice above, this book will also provide counsel on important topics, such as these:

- Navigating your shifting relationships in the workplace and at home

- Developing resilience and grace in the face of your inevitable screw-ups

- Integrating #MeToo and #BlackLivesMatter principles into your leadership style
- Embracing your impact and newfound power in your community

As you can see, this book seeks to nurture both your soul and your mind, instead of solely focusing on numbers and rules. My goal is to escort you into this new position of power in a more ethereal way, while simultaneously challenging you to explore what makes you unique.

I welcome you on this journey, where I will share what I've learned in my years of managing Homo sapiens—the good, the bad, and the ugly—so you can enter this new role as the badass you clearly are.

Now that you know what you're getting into (and you can't hop off the ride now), buckle your seatbelt.

It's officially time to boss up, buttercup!

chapter 2

YOU'VE JUST BEEN PROMOTED. NOW WHAT?

"…each of us has a personal calling…the best way to succeed is to discover what you love and then find a way to offer it to others in the form of service…"
—Oprah Winfrey

You just got promoted to the exclusive-yet-alluring club of people managers?! HUGE FUCKING CONGRATULATIONS for starters! I fondly remember the day myself—it was the same day the San Francisco Giants won the World Series, so a couple big things happened that day. I called my family to tell them as I stood out on the fire escape of my shoebox apartment in San Francisco's SOMA district, smoking a cigarette (which was a thing I used to do when I wanted to pretend I was Carrie Bradshaw), and thought about my perfect, ambitious life with a shit-eating grin, looking down at the streets as the city erupted in spontaneous celebration when the Giants win was broadcast. In my mind, I pretended they were celebrating my promotion.

Now, I don't recommend hanging out on sketchy fire escapes or smoking (seriously, don't take it up; it's very bad for you), but you absolutely should stop what you're doing right now and go celebrate. For real, though—this is a huge deal and before you start really getting into it, you should take a night or two and really enjoy the satisfaction of this promotion.

I'm not kidding. Get out there and celebrate. Make that LinkedIn post, have that froyo with your colleagues or that Jägermeister shot with your BFF. Treat yourself with those new shoes or watch or ice cream or whatever! The important thing is to do something to give yourself accolades for this incredibly huge accomplishment.

And don't forget to give thanks to those who helped get you here—whether it be mentors, teachers, role models, community members, friends, or family. You are a conglomeration of all those who have influenced your journey, so make sure to share the moment with those who helped make it all possible.

So, did you go out and celebrate? Read on to see what's next! If you didn't, put this book down right now and go do so. You'll regret it if you don't.

Beyond it being fun, delicious, or relaxing, it's also super important to take these moments to celebrate your own personal achievements. Doing so will not only set a great example for the team you're about to inherit or hire (because you want them to celebrate their achievements and feel proud, too), but also because . . .

Your life is about to get really tough.

I hate to be the one to break it to you, but the reality is that your world is about to get turned upside down—for the better, mind you—but you really should be bracing yourself for about six to nine months of bizarro world. But don't worry. This book is intended to be your guide for this somewhat painful transition, and it's going to be a lot smoother if you know that going in. Mental preparedness is key here!

Enjoy the newfound influence and (most likely) the raise! But brace yourself. You'll soon find out why managers get paid more.

Here are a few changes you can expect to see, seemingly overnight, that are about to define your work world:

- Time to divorce your work spouses
- The Big Picture
- The metrics have changed big-time
- Welcome to the insiders' clubhouse

TIME TO DIVORCE YOUR WORK SPOUSES

"If you can't say something good about someone, sit right here by me"
—Alice Roosevelt Longworth[2]

Say goodbye to your days of work gossip (and don't pretend you won't miss it).

I get it. Our highest self knows that gossip is toxic, but deep down, we've all got a little basic bitch in us that just loves to chitchat about our coworkers over pumpkin spice lattes.

But not anymore.

Emotionally detaching from your friends at work is one of the first new behaviors you should immediately incorporate into your day-to-day conduct, as your every action will have a lasting impact on your effectiveness over the long run. This shift can be one of the hardest to adopt, because, to be honest, it can feel lonely.

But you have to do it, for several reasons:

- There's a new hierarchy
- You got the job; they didn't
- Confidentiality = trust
- Secrets, secrets, secrets

First and foremost, if you were promoted amongst peers to lead a team of employees who were previously at your reporting level, your relation to the group has changed, so how you carry yourself needs to change as well. It's

---

2 Jean Vanden Heuvel, "The Sharpest Wit in Washington," the Saturday Evening Post, December 4, 1965.

critical to take an emotional step back from the social aspect of your workplace to establish yourself as a leader. This will feel awkward and maybe even a little painful at first.

In any preexisting friendships you may have had on your team, your new relationship to them as their manager has to take priority. These individuals whom you care about need you to be a good and accountable manager for them, more than they need their manager to be their friend. Think of it in the same way children need their parents to be parents (at least in their younger years), not friends. Just like kids don't need a "cool mom" (sorry, Regina George), your employees don't need a "cool manager."

Beyond this change being necessary for the betterment of your team and employees, some of your peers may have applied and been rejected from the promotion you just got. Because of all the disappointment and frustration they're likely feeling from the move, it may be difficult for both of you to form a positive working relationship at first.

The most important thing in cases like these is that these individuals feel comfort and reliability from you despite the awkwardness and competitiveness. You want them to recognize you have the best of intentions, are going to be a terrific manager for them, and may even help them reach their professional goals. In order to achieve this kind of trust, it will be critical that they view you as a true leader and not just as so-and-so's happy hour confidant.

Additionally, every single one of your new team members needs to trust that your confidentiality and impartiality are of utmost priority—otherwise, they won't be able to come to you with a problem. It's just not possible to establish this while maintaining the same social connections with the team.

Resist the urge to engage in any gossip or excessive socializing with existing friends at work. Your first task is to establish yourself as a boss, not a friend, to your team and new colleagues.

Lastly, when you become a manager, you will be privy to sensitive human resources (HR) and company information that you'll need to keep to yourself, such as the intentions of your board to acquire another company, possible future funding information, or the fact that the company's CTO had a tough personal issue that is affecting the morale of the engineering department. You don't want anyone, including your supervisors, thinking you can't be trusted.

It's a critical step to take in order to effectively negotiate and navigate within the upper ranks of the company on behalf of your team. This will take time, of course, but the first priority is to evaluate and consciously embrace an aloofness from your existing friendships to give yourself the space to move through this transition.

Phew! I know that is a lot to take in.

While everything outlined above is very true and important, I also want to emphasize that this social isolation is not necessarily a dynamic you'll need to maintain in the long run. Eventually, you'll be able to switch between "friend mode" and "boss mode" more fluidly—also, reentering these friendships may just look and feel different while you remain colleagues.

To get on the right foot and ensure a healthy start to your new relationship with your team, I suggest prioritizing the following:

1. Within 36 to 48 hours from your first day or when your promotion is announced, **schedule a casual chat or check-in with each employee you'll be directly managing.** I recommend giving them a full day to process the news on their own, so typically try to schedule this a day or so out. Make it clear in your communications about this meeting that this won't be formal, but rather it will be a casual getting-to-know-you chitchat. Know that their anxiety may be at a 10 after they find out about you, and they will undoubtedly feel somewhat cautious about this new arrangement.

2. Show your new team members that you're invested in their success and in the relationship from the get-go by **asking questions about both their professional background and goals, as well as their personal life.** Write down details they share with you about their family lives, such as the name of their spouses or partners, any pets they have, and names and ages of their children. Remembering personal details like these will go far in establishing a warmth in your relationship and a personal connection in addition to the work itself.

3. In addition to discussions about the work, in your first few days it's good to **invest some time in building a casual rapport with your new team members** outside of any preordained one-on-ones or meetings. Great examples of this are sending them a little joke about the weather, giving an update on a Netflix show you know you both watch, or asking them about their plans for an upcoming weekend. Establishing more casual communication norms in addition to the regular formal

ones will show that you're approachable. And because you establish that comfort, your team members will be more likely to open up and share concerns about work that you'll need to know.

Say goodbye to the sweet, sweet wine of workplace gossip, and, if needed, replace it with some great reality TV shows to scratch your itch. Your team needs you!

THE BIG PICTURE

"Tell me, what is it you plan to do with your one wild and precious life?"
—Mary Oliver[3]

Folks, we're going to go a little deep on this one. Are you ready to zoom out?

As a millennial, you are probably already an overthinker, sensitive, a little anxious, always on the verge of an existential crisis, and addicted to your phone. If so, you are the perfect leader for the moment. The world needs people like you, badly, to shape a better future for all of us. In this new role, your sphere of influence has now exploded, and the impact you leave should be one you're proud of.

On an emotional level, you are probably observing a shift in your world-view and your understanding of your place in the world. Overnight, you have been put in a place of power and privilege with an enormous amount of responsibility. You now have the ability to affect the day-to-day lives of not only your direct reports, but also their families and any customers or projects they're working with or on, your company's strategy, your own family and community, and the list goes on and on.

---

3 Mary Oliver, "Poem 133: The Summer Day," in New and Selected Poems: Volume One (Boston, MA: Beacon Press, 2004).

Really, your entire reality has changed in one day, and it's important to be both humble and confident in that change.

Take a minute to reflect on your newfound power and influence.
It's a big deal.

Remember, if you're here, it's because you've earned it. You've been identified as a natural leader and have been chosen by people you respect to lead, and that's a big deal. You've been trusted with the careers and livelihoods of your team and their ability to take care of their families and to advance in their own profession, which is no small matter.

To break this down further, allow me to illustrate with a series of visuals.

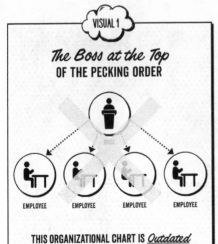

This organizational chart shows the leader at the top of the chart, indicating the flow of power from their platform to the subservient employees who take orders and execute. It is accurate in reporting structure, but incomplete in capturing the sphere of influence that you now wield.

The servant-leader model has become a more popular emotional representation of the role of a manager. While I appreciate the sentiment of this visualization, I think it falls short of acknowledging the responsibility and role of a true leader—which, yes, is partly to serve, but from a position of strength, power, and humility.

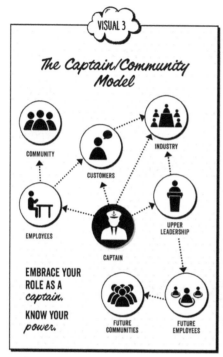

VISUAL 3

The Captain/Community Model

COMMUNITY

CUSTOMERS

INDUSTRY

EMPLOYEES

CAPTAIN

UPPER LEADERSHIP

EMBRACE YOUR ROLE AS A *captain.* KNOW YOUR *power.*

FUTURE COMMUNITIES

FUTURE EMPLOYEES

This last visualization is the one I'd encourage you to adopt. As a manager, you don't actually have control of anything just because someone reports to you at work.

What you have is *influence.*

You are at the center of many more lives than just those who are on your team. Their families, communities, and future careers are all now within your span of impact, and this reality should not be taken lightly.

Seemingly overnight, you're at the core of a vast universe.

If you don't believe me, think back to the bosses you've had over the years and how you remember—in excruciating detail—the conversations you had with them. How much did they influence your quality of life, for better or for worse?

Then, recall the people who you interacted with and who influenced you during that time. That's right—the mentorship you received is still having an impact on you today. Likewise, the impact you can have on your circle can have a similar exponential effect, and some of that influence you won't ever see or even know about.

And now, you're the one with that power. Sit with that for a minute.

You might even be thinking at this point, Well, *shit! What should I do with this power? How do I handle this moral crisis? What if I ruin someone's life?*

If these questions are on your mind, it's because you are taking your role seriously, and that's a good thing! The more you recognize the immense power and influence you have, the more apt you'll be to wield it responsibly and effectively.

We'll get there, but for now, just sit with it.

Wow!

THE METRICS HAVE CHANGED

"A leader is best when people barely know he exists. When his work is done, his aim fulfilled, they will say: we did it ourselves."
—Laozi [4]

A few weeks after the screaming phone call from my newly promoted friend, my phone blew up with a slew of DMs from her. My immediate response was to glance at the calendar. Just as I'd suspected, it had been a few weeks since her initial promotion—she was in the Crash 'n' Burn phase.

Uh oh, I thought, I'd better give her a call.

Unlike the 2004 racing game of the same name, the Crash 'n' Burn phase is not something Kyle will be playing while drinking Monster. So, what is it?

The Crash 'n' Burn is the term I've coined for the *lowwww* point that usually comes right after the honeymoon phase of a first-time manager job. It's usually characterized by aggressive performance anxiety, crippling

---

4   Laozi, *Tao Te Ching*, chapter 17, 4th century BC.

imposter syndrome, and a less-than-impressive first few weeks in the new role. Ultimately, it's a result of the growing pain of realizing—and fully internalizing—that your entire world has changed.

Suddenly, your success is inextricably linked to your team's output. Put another way, your professional impact and results are now measured by your team's delivery, not your own. That's a tough concept to grasp. At times, you may even be forced to make some tough decisions about how to spend your time.

But be careful!

In the past, you probably produced some impressive results, but you now have to make some tradeoffs between your own work and the needs of your team. About nine times out of 10, I recommend prioritizing your team, especially during your first 90 days acclimating to this new position.

Reading through my friend's messages, it was evident she was struggling with this. "I feel like I'm doing okay-ish as a manager and pretty shitty as a marketing contributor," I read. "I used to be at the top of my game, but now I'm only reaching the bare minimum."

This is a constant tug-of-war most new managers face. My advice to her, and now to you, is to let some of your personal work slip if you have to. Don't let it fail, but you'll be in a world of hurt if you don't hit the ground running as a manager and set a strong leadership style and relationship with your team.

At best, you'll have to re-establish authority and trust after missing that critical 90-day window while completely burning yourself out. At worst, your team will find opportunities with stronger managers elsewhere, forcing you to now pick up their work in addition to the work you were already struggling to do.

It's a vicious, vicious cycle, and I recommend allowing yourself to drop the ball a little bit on your personal work at the outset.

For another example, say you're in sales and you recently got promoted to sales manager. You now oversee your team's book of business, but because you're still doing your old job until those accounts get transitioned or you hire your replacement, it's going to be difficult to keep up with those accounts while taking on your new manager responsibilities at the same time.

Stop. Don't let those accounts completely implode, but accept that you're not going to be doing as good a job with them as you could before.

Think of it this way: Not only are you responsible for doing all of your work, but you now also have to monitor the quality and output of work across your entire team—meaning, you'll have to answer for any and all projects within your team's scope. With that in mind, does spending so much time on your own personal work still make sense? Probably not.

This new reality is a big shift in perspective and will take some time to fully absorb. But trust me when I say it's one of the most common management newbie mistakes to prioritize personal work over the team's work— and it's very hard to come back stronger from it. So, get used to the fact that your team's output is now what you're being measured against, but also what you'll take some credit for down the line.

WELCOME TO THE CLUBHOUSE—PULL UP A CHAIR!

"I didn't feel sad or happy. I didn't feel proud or ashamed. I only felt that in spite of all the things I'd done wrong, in getting myself here, I'd done right."
—Cheryl Strayed [5]

We've all had that experience with a less-than-effective manager who made us want to pull our hair out. For me, it was my first manager out of college. Micromanaging was this person's forte, and our relationship grew strained from it. I spent the first two years of my career basically convinced I was a terrible employee with no real significant career potential after having internalized their condescension quite extensively. Our relationship was so toxic that it devolved into a literal shouting and crying episode in the parking lot of our workplace one night—something I don't recommend.

It turns out I wasn't the only person unhappy with this particular leader's work performance, and they were eventually fired from the company on a technicality (I think they were lying on expense reports or something). There had been many complaints over the years, but this person's removal from the company ultimately came swiftly and from upper management.

My former boss's response was to leave a dead fish to rot inside the person's desk who had terminated their employment. Yikes and yikes. Working for this manager was a wild ride, and while you can certainly consider yourself successful as a manager if you've never opened your desk to discover lutefisk in your top drawer from an angry ex-employee, that is a very low barometer that you will surely surpass.

---

5   Cheryl Strayed, *Wild: A Journey from Lost to Found* (London, UK: Atlantic Books, 2012).

But I digress. What is your management horror story? If you're like most people, you would cite micromanaging as one of the main causes for this frustration. While that may very well be true, chances are, there's more drama going on behind the scenes that is making that particular leader flounder (fish jokes aside), which is, in turn, making all of their employees miserable. That drama you may not have perceived at the time was likely due to their inability to function as a leader within the upper circles of management at the company, so they exert all this frustration towards their team in a sad but desperate attempt to ensure the work is getting done despite their incompetence.

When leaders aren't effective in establishing healthy and functional working dynamics with their new leadership teams, especially those in a horizontal layer across the company, the team suffers. If your relationship with the clubhouse isn't fostered properly, it can cause your team to feel isolated from the broader company culture, out of alignment with the mission, and/or confused about its priorities.

Compounding the problem is a common issue we discussed earlier: New leaders struggle to navigate the shift in their personal relationships and spend a disproportionate amount of time spinning their wheels there. It can get to the point where the new manager becomes too depleted to engage with their team.

The result of both dynamics can often be a tendency to micromanage, because these leaders haven't positioned their team in a place to execute effectively without daily direction.

Now, let's discuss how to avoid this outcome so *you* don't become the micromanaging boss that so many employees complain about! First of all, what is it going to *feel* like to move up in the ranks of the org chart?

For starters, your Slack is going to have a few more notifications now that you're a manager, and so will your LinkedIn messages.

You'll get pulled into new meetings you weren't previously privy to, you'll have a moment when you more openly discuss salaries across levels with other managers, and your HR system will update to visibly show your position and direct reporting relationships.

You'll probably be involved automatically in new conversations, email threads, and chat groups. You might even be warmly pulled to new networks with a different caliber of coworker than you are used to.

Furthermore, after you move into management, you'll get the sudden sensation that you're part of some exclusive club. Even more strange is the fact that those in your personal life will notice that.

Seemingly overnight, you may be treated differently by peers, your own manager, and even friends and family. It can be thrilling, but it ends up being emotionally awkward and draining. I found that I was getting hit up for jobs or introductions from friends down on their luck, and suddenly got a lot of requests in my network for "coffee" or asks to be mentored.

Be excited…and cautious!

You probably got into a management career because you love helping others and enjoy bringing people up with you, but you'll need to curate your time outside of work a bit more thoughtfully now that you're about to have a *lot* more on your plate. I even recommend having a canned response ready to go, something like, "Thank you for reaching out! I've got some really ambitious projects right now with my new role, so I don't have bandwidth to connect at this time."

It may feel bad at first, but you'll feel even worse by spreading yourself too thin these first few months in your new role.

When I was first promoted to manager, I was struck by so many things. Suddenly, there were new software packages I could use and new information I could access, such as the amount my team was making, their previous performance reports, and new manager-only Slack channels. There were manager-level meetings, happy hours, and other functions I was expected to attend.

From day one, you are going to have access to a new and different network. Establish yourself in this new circle but listen and learn what the dynamic is ...and who's who.

As you navigate your way through these new social circles, make your presence known. Find the perfect balance between asserting your influence and taking time to listen and assess who's who. Detect who the true influencers are in your new circles versus who may be there by title only. To be an effective leader, you'll need to form a lot of important connections so you can pull strings with others when necessary.

You should also exercise extreme caution as you learn sensitive company information and compensation details about your new team. Remember, you cannot use this new intel in any way to benefit yourself. For example, if you find out one of your direct reports makes more than you, that's *not* a negotiating tactic. Don't ever talk about other people's salaries, company secrets, or other sensitive information with your team, because your ability to be trustworthy is a one-shot deal. If you screw it up, it's over. So, don't screw it up.

When you move into management, it can feel like gaining access to an exclusive members-only club. You have my permission to let it go to your head a little—you are a VIP now! But be thoughtful, strong, and conscious about how you approach these new social groups.

Here are some ideas for adjusting to this new normal in a more concrete way:

- Develop a canned response for **politely declining invitations to socialize or network in ways that you feel will deplete your focus and energy.** You'll have more time for these types of meetings later, but for now you have to focus. You can say, for example, "Thanks for the invitation! I just took on a new role at work and have some ambitious priorities, so I have to decline this for now."

- Set up a coffee or other casual **meet-and-greet with a cross-functional selection of your peers, especially leaders of departments** in which your team regularly depends on or collaborates with. Establishing these connections up front sets you up to work seamlessly with other leaders, so your team feels in lockstep with broader company initiatives.

- **Seek community with other leaders in similar roles** or in your industry outside of your company. Find and network with groups of peers, even if they are internet-only contacts, to surround and support you with ideas and lessons learned so you have a support system outside of your direct peers.

- In your personal life, **prioritize and nurture the most important relationships in your support network,** such as your inner circle of friends. If necessary, reassure them that you are still present and invested in those relationships, even if for the next few months you might seem less available. Call to let people know you're alive.

Once you adjust to your new responsibilities and workload, you'll have more emotional energy to be more present.

- If you have a partner, **discuss openly the challenges you expect during the next few months and support you'll need during this time.** It's okay if you don't know exactly what that is yet and if those needs change over time. Be intentional about keeping a boundary for both parts of your life, and avoid the temptation to discuss the personal, private matters of your team members with your partner.

Buckle up! You'll need to reorient yourself to new peers, managers, and networks, so take in as much as you can and enjoy the ride.

chapter 3

THE BASICS: EXPENSES, HIRING, PTO, AND MANAGEMENT HANDOFF

Your alarm shocks you out of bed. Nearly hyperventilating, you realize it's the first Monday of your new role. After you do your morning routine—walk the dog, do a HIIT workout, shower—you settle into your desk and boot up your computer, ready to hit the proverbial ground running in your new fancy job.

The first thing you do is check your calendar. There, you notice you have a few hours free in the afternoon, and you furrow your eyebrows in confusion. You may be experiencing one of the strange realities of your new role: Oftentimes, managers have more free time because their individual project work has decreased (or soon will).

For A-types like us, it can produce anxiety to think about how to use this time. So, what do you actually do with your time now?

This chapter is intended to help new managers figure out what their immediate tactical priorities should be on day one, in order of what is most crucial.

When I was first promoted, I happened to be at a quickly growing, but still small, tech startup where the HR function was still in its early days. For that reason, we had to teach ourselves the ropes of management quickly.

At first, I was inheriting only two direct reports and still functioning in a hybrid player-coach role—my own ongoing responsibilities still critical and expected. With this ramp into full-time management, I had a little time to get my bearings before I had to go into full swing.

Just two months later, my team swelled from two to five, and then doubled to 10 by the end of the year, so the precious time I had with my small team proved very helpful in figuring out what I needed to prioritize.

I learned that these are the four most important operational checklist priorities:

- Financials (expenses and such)
- Hiring
- PTO
- Management handoff

Let's start with everyone's favorite, expense reports!

IT'S ALL ABOUT THE BENJAMINS, BABY

"Money does not make you happy but it quiets the nerves."
—Unknown

A few years into my management career, the time had come to promote two of my team members to front-line managers as I ascended to the director role. I was so excited to guide them through their journey to Team Management, and I couldn't wait to hear about how their first few days had gone in this new role. Thinking back, I was amused to receive text messages from both of them about how excited they were to have an expense report to approve (hah!). This arbitrary-but-not-insignificant milestone does have a way of making things feel official, somehow.

But if they had only known what else was about to hit them!

I'm starting with expense reports, not because they're the sexiest of management duties, but also because doing them is a responsibility you'll probably encounter from day one and may require immediate action, depending on the cash flow needs of your team and how your organization deals with them.

These might feel tedious…or like a small thrill!

Suddenly, you're in charge of approving money transactions (yay!). But remember that you don't want to eff this one up. Being the reason that somebody wasn't able to make their mortgage payment or overdrew their bank account is a terrible thing. You never really know the financial and cash flow situation of your team members, so it's best to assume that quickly unblocking expense reimbursement will be more than welcomed.

You also don't want to hurt your credibility as a new manager by giving guidance on something that you assumed was reimbursable, like an employee's home office or a drink for a client, but it turned out not to be. Asking your new team member to swallow that cost would be a terribly bad offense. It's easy to get expense reports down, but a stupid thing to screw up—so don't!

It may seem trivial, but figuring out expenses right away will help establish your credibility.

The first thing you're going to want to do is check with your HR department and management cohort to learn your organization's best practices and expense-related software operations. Do this right away, because it will vary wildly depending on your industry and role. I've seen everything from policies where individuals turned in physical receipts within some sort of envelope that eventually got billed to the client, to systems where employees received a per diem payout that they spent however they saw fit.

Here are a few items you should check for in your company's expense policy (not an exhaustive list):

- Home office expenses

- Client entertainment (such as food and alcohol)

- Individual software license, if needed (such as SurveyMonkey)

- Cell phone expenses

- Home internet

- Mileage for work-related travel

- Gift cards as prizes for team events or for celebrations (such as birthdays) [6]

You should also establish a general approach to expenses with your team, so that you have no surprises.

Do you want your team to run these by you before requesting payouts? Is there a certain threshold for the dollar amount you prefer preapproving? What is your sentiment about travel expenses—do you prefer when your team is more comfortable and presumably more productive, or do you enforce a strict budget? What if you have a working lunch and one person picks up the tab—does each person need to submit their own receipt, or is one receipt with everyone's names sufficient? Do you want your team to gather up and turn in receipts logged to specific clients or projects, or just aggregated at month's end and sent in a batch?

This will probably vary a bit based on how your departments' cost centers work and how the expenses are classified in your financial statements, so figure it out!

---

6   Be careful with gift cards in the workplace. They can often create a nightmare headache for payroll, who technically has to go and tax the gift cards, while gift cards as gifts to clients is also slightly fraught because of bribing, etc. For more, see here: https://www.lexology.com/library/detail.aspx?g=a16f15d9-d2e6-431a-a2e9-bfa94ac445f9 and https://stratus.hr/2019/04/12/employee-gift-card-taxable/.

The answers to these questions will be partly your own personal style, and partly made in coordination with your leader and HR or finance functions. But, however it plays out, you should learn this aspect of your role quickly to establish norms on spending and avoid awkward conversations. Your team should feel confident spending what they need to get their jobs done, while you should prioritize understanding how to get them paid back so you aren't the reason that they might have a cash flow crunch.

In sum, read up on your company's expense policy, discuss best practices with your own manager, and make it very clear to your team how this should be handled. Then, you can move on to some of the fun stuff!

YOUR FIRST HIRE

"I was always self-conscious about the fact that I didn't have as much comedy experience as other people at SNL, and I kept thinking they were going to realize they'd made a mistake by hiring me."
—Bill Hader[7]

Imagine if you were the talent scout who had discovered Bill Hader!

One of the most important responsibilities (and opportunities to prove yourself) you'll have is hiring. Depending on what kind of workload your team has, the growth rate of your company, and a variety of other factors, you might need to start thinking about hiring *immediately*.

Seriously—don't miss the boat here. Hiring is one of the aspects of your new job that is almost always going to feel nonurgent. The process is long and it requires methodical and emotionally invested efforts, but if it's done

---

7   Ree Hines, "Bill Hader suffered panic attacks on 'Saturday Night Live,'" TODAY, August 15, 2013, https://www.today.com/popculture/bill-hader-suffered-panic-attacks-saturday-night-live-6C10928323.

poorly, hiring can dog your success as a new manager during the most important time when you're earning your chops. A bad hire is one of the hardest-to-correct mistakes that managers make, so while it might not *feel* like something you should prioritize early on, trust me when I say that you don't want to make the mistake of delaying the process.

As with expenses, you'll need to quickly learn your company's policies and procedures for hiring rapidly. Get acquainted with your hiring partners (if any) and talk to them about how to best work together. Read—thoroughly—your company's handbook with your new lens of having to speak to it with candidates.

For example, you should be able to state at the drop of a hat what your company's stock-matching vesting schedule is, so that you are able to quickly orient prospective candidates to their total compensation package. And, of course, your new prospective employees will also get the benefit of working for you, so be confident in the value you bring to the table!

Familiarize yourself with your company's general policies on the following:

- General compensation structures and levels
- 401(k) matching
- Health-care coverage for employees and their dependents
- Parental leave
- Onboarding checklists
- New-hire orientation materials
- Tuition reimbursement
- Relocation reimbursement
- Home office provisions

Furthermore, once you've figured out who your hiring partners are, try to understand what the growth plan is for your department. Do you have any open head count, any potential internal transfers, or any potential attrition?

In other words, see if you can assess right now how aggressively you may have to hire.

Even though you should always be thinking about hiring no matter what your current head-count situation is, planning for it in advance will help you organize your time from the get-go. You never know when you'll suddenly have a spot or when someone will leave the organization and you'll need to quickly backfill.

Be careful!

A new manager trap is to let the newfound glory of this sudden infusion of power go to your head. Your first hiring decision will be one of your most important tests as a manager, so it's not something to take lightly. You'll want to show everyone you can conduct this process in a fair, efficient, and collaborative way, so avoid the temptation to call all your friends or former coworkers and offer them a job or to give any indication to anyone that you'll now be in a position to hire them.

Similarly, remember in the previous chapter how I introduced the idea of your social network starting to shift? Now that you're in a position to hire people, some of your friends will start asking you for jobs, or they'll want to make introductions to their friends looking for jobs. Maybe they're not even being that direct about it and are asking you for a cryptic "coffee meetup."

I remember being somewhat thrown off by some of my acquaintance relationships starting to feel a bit more…thirsty, shall we say? Having been on the other side of things, I recognize and appreciate the hustle. Just prepare yourself for doing a lot of listening.

My best advice: Approach these invitations with intrigue and caution. Work towards a balance of open-mindedness and detached empathy for people in your network trying to find a job, but have some canned talking points about your hiring plans and practices at your company. Although it may feel emotionally satisfying to be able to help a friend in this way, you'll need to be thoughtful in how you make these critical first decisions about how you're conducting the hiring process. Likewise, if you work in an industry that struggles with lack of diversity and representation (which is probably all of them), you'll want to take extra care to be thoughtful with this decision.

We'll go over how to build diverse, inclusive teams a bit later, but the big takeaway here is that you should consciously reflect on how your new-found power to offer jobs is also an enormous responsibility.

Figure out hiring responsibilities ASAP, but don't let this newfound power go to your head.

So, immediately after you figure out expenses, you should determine if there are any candidates who are at some stage in the hiring process that you'll need to manage. Check with your hiring partners to assess what is in flight and what, if anything, you'll need to do to facilitate the next steps.

If you do hiring right (and you will!), you just may find the next Bill Hader of your industry!

TIME TO THINK ABOUT TIME OFF: DEALING WITH PTO AND LEAVE

"You lack a foot to travel? Then journey into yourself—that leads to transformation of dust into pure gold.."
—Rumi

I don't think it was possible for me to write this book without quoting the Sufi mystic Rumi at least once, and this section may as well be it.

One of the likely scenarios you'll be dealing with on day one (or two or three) is approving vacation requests so your wonderful new team can embrace life to its fullest, recharge their spirits, and generate lifelong family memories. Fun! Fun?

It can be fun, but let's also consider your responsibility to keep the train on the tracks while not forgetting the inevitability of *unexpected* leave—not fun stuff. Like it or not, in addition to the fun leave that is PTO, you will be dealing with sudden absences when, for example, an employee resigns, experiences a health crisis, or has a family emergency. Keeping the train on the tracks, granting needed PTO, and keeping the business operational on top of it all can be quite the challenge!

To demonstrate the tough choices you'll have to make, let's take the examples of hypothetical managers Sally and Ricardo.

Sally is a nurse manager in a Level 1 Trauma Center in Detroit, Michigan. For Sally, staff time off is just not available when people need a recharge. In an industry such as emergency medicine where a certain level of staffing is required to operate safely, managing PTO requires the same level of precision that is applied to patient care.

Ricardo is an engineering manager at a large cloud-hosting company with a pager duty setup for his infrastructure team, which hosts data for some of the country's top financial institutions. Any miniscule issue with the servers can cause the banking systems to screech to a halt. Ricardo obviously needs to pay close attention to managing PTO to avoid even the possibility of disruption to business operations. Ricardo also knows the criticality of time off, because the intense problem-solving nature of his infrastructure team requires creativity, relaxation, and a sense of balance.

For Sally and Ricardo, approving PTO isn't just a matter of opinion or culture. It's a matter of life, death, or financial crisis.

Regardless of what type of industry you're in, you'll need to quickly gain an understanding of your organization's policy and approach towards PTO and other types of leave, as well as the ongoing operations of your department and what staffing levels are generally needed to maintain continuity.

You'll also need to quickly establish norms for requesting vacation, and communicate your preferences with your team up front. This can be a somewhat uncomfortable and difficult topic to sort out with your direct reports, because it is largely going to be determined by your industry's norms.

Here are some questions about time off to ask yourself and discuss with your new team:

- Do you want your team to send you a calendar invite before requesting specific days off?

- Do you prefer discussing PTO plans in a one-on-one?

- Do you want your team to consult a shared calendar and work amongst themselves to determine reasonable coverage schedules?

- Are your team members responsible for their own coverage, or are you the default backup for your team members' PTO?

- Do you expect your team to simply take the time they need, even when you know they have specific deliverables they're responsible for meeting (like a sales number)?

If your workplace offers any other kind of leave, such as parental leave, sabbaticals, or flextime, make sure you familiarize yourself with those policies. Also: take note of what time has already been requested and granted prior to your taking the reins.

Like salary, PTO can be one of those tricky areas where there may be a bit of an ongoing tug-of-war between the business and the employees. Generally, most of your new team members will want to take more PTO than is available, while your direct reports will want to make more money than you can pay them. Meanwhile, you want to make sure your team is getting enough time off to recharge and come ready to do their best work. For these reasons, it can be a tricky process to navigate, especially when you're new.

One important note about time away: Always, always talk to HR in situations like an employee needing more than three consecutive sick days, or when a team member needs to go on short-term disability or bereavement leave. These norms will vary widely company to company and industry to industry, but this can become a giant headache for you, your team member, and HR if you are not keeping them up-to-date. Worst-case scenario is when HR has to tell your employees that you were wrong or uninformed because you weren't crystal clear on legal leave. As a rule of thumb, anything beyond straight-up vacation time within allotted vacation allowances should involve a conversation with HR.

From day one on the job, you'll have to learn the balance of managing the scarcity of PTO with the needs of the business.

That being said, take your own PTO and make sure your team uses theirs. Remember that the mind's creativity thrives in unstructured time away from core responsibilities. After all, Lin-Manuel Miranda conceived of Hamilton while on freakin' vacation![8]

---

8   Anna Almendrala, "Lin-Manuel Miranda: It's 'No Accident' Hamilton Came To Me On Vacation," Huff Post, June 23, 2016, https://www.huffpost.com/entry/lin-manuel-miranda-says-its-no-accident-hamilton-inspiration-struck-on-vacation_n_576c136ee4b0b489bb0ca7c2.

MANAGEMENT HANDOFF

*"You wanna know what scares people? Success. When you don't make
moves and you don't climb up the ladder, everybody loves you
because you're not competition."*
—Nicki Minaj [9]

Nicki Minaj knows a thing or two about success. A product of the quintessential American dream, she was born in Trinidad and grew up in poverty in Queens, New York. Driven by her desire to take care of her mother despite her father's abuse and neglect, Nicki hustled her way to success, step by step. She scored herself gig after gig singing backup for rappers in New York, eventually writing her own music and attracting the attention of Dirty Money CEO Fendi.

By 2010, she had released her first single, "Massive Attack," and just a couple of months later, she won Best Female Hip-Hop Artist at the BET Awards. Nicki's strong moral compass, tenacity, and fierce independence were crucial factors in her quest to overcome her tough childhood and change the hip-hop game forever.[10]

When you first take the reins of management, you'll need to channel your inner Nicki Minaj as you embrace your newfound success and take stock of your new empire. (By your empire, I obviously mean your department!) If you don't, you risk losing precious onboarding time by having to build your own mental model of how the team works. Then, you'll lose access to any helpful insights on existing structures, culture, and expectations that a previous manager might have provided.

---

9   Mariel Concepcion, "Nicki Minaj Says Lil Kim Will Be Remembered As 'Sore Loser,'" Billboard, November 22, 2010, https://www.billboard.com/articles/columns/the-juice/950487/nicki-minaj-says-lil-kim-will-be-remembered-as-sore-loser.
10   Sara Ryan, "Inside Nicki Minaj's Sad Real-Life Story," The List, June 4, 2020, https://www.thelist.com/215101/inside-nicki-minajs-sad-real-life-story/.

Likely, you've just inherited something from someone. It's up to you to quickly assess your team's previous management situation and soak in as much info as you can from the previous manager you are taking the reins from. This can be tricky depending on the circumstances of the management structure prior to your team's formation, but however it came to be, you'll want to act very quickly to get information that's still fresh in the previous manager's mind.

If you got promoted into management from a previous team leader role, it's possible that you are still reporting to the same individual your peers were previously reporting into. Therefore, you are now the only one who is still reporting to the former team manager. This can feel like a complicated situation, as you'll now need to adjust to this new team dynamic carefully and over time. So, as soon as your promotion happens, make sure to prioritize speaking candidly with your boss about any hard-earned wisdom they have gained.

Extract detailed information from them about the following:

- Performance
- Pay history
- Performance history
- Other relevant information, such as career goals and interests

It's smart to provide as much continuity as possible regarding the information you learned from any goal-setting and coaching conversations, but also trust that you'll be able to bring a fresh perspective and new energy to those conversations.

If you are inheriting a team from a manager who is moving to another role in the company, take advantage of still having access to that manager and pick their brain while you can. Ask many of the same questions about performance, history, etc. as in the previous situation, but you'll need to be slightly more cautious and discreet in these circumstances.

And here's where it can get...sticky.

You may need to channel your inner Nicki here. You may not know the full backstory of why the previous manager is transitioning to another role, so take things with a grain of salt a bit more and validate what you are hearing with other trusted managers in your department or company, if possible.

It could very well be that this manager was asked to move on, is transitioning due to poor management feedback, or something else. You'll have to lean on your professional judgement a bit more in these cases and make sure to talk things out with your own new manager to get additional viewpoints.

Alternatively, you could be coming into a situation where you have little to no management-handoff opportunities for a variety of reasons. These can be very messy situations, but they can also be beneficial in some ways.

On one hand, you may be inheriting a team that was poorly managed. Your direct reports will be frustrated at having to start over with any feedback and career conversations they've had with the previous management, and you may have a troubling personnel situation brewing under the surface that will take you awhile to figure out without having much contact with previous managers.

On the other hand, you'll have the opportunity to start fresh and energize the team without having any previous notions of what you're coming into, so that could be a blessing in disguise.

Whatever the situation is, learn as much information as you can but be careful not to adopt those viewpoints as your own. Any opinions of previous managers are valuable because of just that—they are the opinions of a previous manager.

Remember that you were hired to lead your team because of your innate abilities to form fair judgements and influence others, so don't feel like you have to continue the playbook of any previous managers to a T. If you can at all, minimize disruption to the day-to-day business, but also don't be afraid to lead with authority and trust your own judgement from day one.

Gather as much insight and information as possible from your team's previous manager, but trust your judgement and chops when you step up to lead.

As an example, here is a spreadsheet template I've used when completing management handoffs and have asked the previous manager to complete in preparation for our transition.

NAME	TITLE	RECOMMEND FOR PROMOTION Y/N	COMP NOTES	FLIGHT RISK?
Joy Santana	Senior Customer Manager	Y	At midpoint for role; recently increased 5% during previous review; suggest 10% for next cycle due to taking on large client	Y
Stephen Robinson	Business Development	N	55k + 30% bonus if partnership quota hit	N
Isaiah Levy	Business Development	N	58k + 30% bonus if partnership quota hit	Y

BUSINESS IMPACT	OTHER NOTES AND CONSIDERATIONS	EMILY'S NOTES FROM FIRST 1:1
High	Joy started as an intern with the company five years ago and has expressed interest in pursuing a higher ed degree. She's personable and ambitious and eager to grow.	Joy mentioned interest in learning more technical skills, and will see if there's a tuition reimbursement option as an alternative to full-time degree if she's interested. Otherwise, will support her to pursue her dreams, but try to get her specialized knowledge distributed across the current team.
Low	Stephen is terrific with sourcing business partnerships but struggles to communicate internally to set up other teams for successful handoff. He will need some work in time management and internal communications in order to expand his career options, which he wants to do.	Stephen seems self-aware of his strengths and weaknesses and indicated he is driven by comp. Wonder if we can restructure his compensation plan to include a bonus if successful partner integrations complete on time, as an example to motivate him to work harder at internal communications.
Low	See related folder of feedback—was rated as "needs improvement" during the last cycle of reviews. Isaiah's performance has been declining ever since being passed up for a promotion.	

Lastly, if your path to management includes being tasked to hire and create a team for the first time, this spreadsheet won't necessarily apply. You'll have the opportunity to create the team how you see fit and have more control over your team's experience with your workplace, which can be easier in some ways, but harder in others. You'll be developing your management chops at the same time as getting an unknown business venture done. In these cases, you'll really want to make sure your hiring decisions are smart since each one has so much impact.

Here is a summary of the most important actions to take to help you in your new role:

- Grab your company handbook and read it *now*, highlighting PTO, leave, and the expense and travel policies.

- Get in touch with your recruiting or HR teams to plug into any in-flight hiring processes and understand what current and future head-count plans are.

- If the previous manager is around, set up a meeting to complete a handoff as soon as you've met one-on-one with your team.

- *Write down everything*, including your initial notes and impressions of your team, anything discussed in person with the previous manager, and any cultural notes shared with you.

The final word goes to Queen Nicki:

"When I'm in the studio, I can't be constantly looking at my phone and, to be honest, I really don't care what other people are doing. When it's time for me to do what I need to do, I know I'm going to be the best, and that's a fact."[11]

---

11 https://en.vogue.me/fashion/all-hail-the-queen-the-nicki-minaj-interview/

chapter 4

THE NOT-SO-BASICS: TEAM MEETINGS, FEEDBACK, AND ESCALATIONS

Congratulations, you've survived the initial shock waves of your promotion!

During your first few days and weeks, you will have sorted out the operating fundamentals necessary to keep the business functioning. Now you're ready to tackle some of the more complex, but incredibly strategic, aspects of your new role. Your success over the long run depends very much on your ability to make a strong start, adapt quickly, and rise to the occasion in your first few weeks, so take care to absorb the topics in this chapter carefully.

We'll start with one of the most important moves you'll make, and that is setting up a—drum roll, please—team meeting! As cheesy as it sounds, this will actually be one of the more impactful actions you'll take to lead by example as you come out of the gate swinging.

Next, we'll dive into another expectation in your new role: feedback. You're probably no stranger to performance feedback, having earned yourself a promotion to management! You've heard the good, the bad, and the ugly from trusted mentors yourself, absorbed it, and then utilized that feedback to transform your skills into your current approach. Well, the tables have turned, my friend. The harsh truth: Your ability to deliver (and receive) quality, thoughtful performance feedback consistently and with grace is now on the line—are you up to the challenge?

Finally, we'll explore your new responsibility as a point of escalation for your team or department. You'll learn how to expect the unexpected, handle client or cross-department nastygrams like a pro, and shield your team from 99 percent of the corporate red tape so that they can focus on their work—and do it all with pizzazz.

Let's do this.

HOW TO MAKE TEAM MEETINGS NOT SUCK

"If you had to identify, in one word, the reason why the human race has not achieved, and never will achieve, its full potential, that word would be 'meetings.'"
—Dave Barry [12]

Most people hate unnecessary meetings. At best, they are a mundane, dry, and painful waste of time and seem to exist only to check an arbitrary operational box in the corporate world. At worst, they are a sizable percentage of our work life that we will never get back, breeding resentment, fatigue, and back-channel grumblings amongst weary participants who would rather be anywhere else.

But they don't have to be.

---

12   Dave Barry, Dave Barry Turns 50 (New York, NY: Ballantine Books, 1999).

How you engage your team and how you approach and set expectations for your team meetings will be an important part of building your team culture and your personal reputation as a leader, so be intentional about it. This is a great and important opportunity to lead by example. Your own personal code of conduct for your team meetings will set the stage for how you expect your team to run their own meetings, both client-facing and internal.

There's no one answer to how to approach these meetings, so don't feel like you have to follow a particular formula or guideline. However, you should consider the norm for your industry and take into account any preexisting team meeting that might still be in place. Depending on how your company is structured, you may also be managing a group of people who aren't exactly a team.

Maybe you're managing people who primarily work on different pods, on specific projects, or even as independent contributors. Don't fall into the trap of thinking, *If my team doesn't really need to collaborate, should I still have a team meeting at all?*

Absolutely.

In those cases, you'll want to really make sure you are using your team time wisely, as your reports won't necessarily need to get together to discuss their day-to-day work as much. Therefore, you may not need to have meetings as frequently, but bringing everyone together at a preset cadence is still beneficial for a few reasons:

1. **Meetings provide social connection.** For many working adults, the workplace has become one of the primary sources of their social life. By creating a sense of belonging within the structure of a meeting, even if informal, you can help facilitate this sense of community.

2. **Meetings provide you with a regular forum to share important company updates.** There will inevitably be messages from your leadership you'll need to relay to your team, and some—such as a transition of an executive, news of a new strategic direction for the company, or insights into what's going on at a leadership level—are best discussed in a group setting.

3. **A regular meeting enables you to carve out time to focus on career development and soft skills or to invest in the well-being of your team.** When business as normal is slow or you don't have any pressing agenda items, your team meeting can be a useful forum for learning a PowerPoint skill together, inviting a member of your copywriting team to teach you how to write better emails, or watching a YouTube meditation tutorial together, for example.

At a recent team meeting for the department I lead, I asked everyone to bring Post-it Notes to the session and write down some of the highlights and lowlights of a recent customer implementation we had all worked on together. After writing down our thoughts, each team member shared their feedback and ideas for improvements with the group.

After the feedback was shared, we took photos of our Post-its and shared in our team chat channel. The notes offered a visual reminder to the team that their thoughts had been heard and validated by their peers and by me. They also provided an unspoken agreement that each person brought a unique and important perspective and that we were all equally accountable to the team for our successes.

Why go through this exercise in a team meeting format?

Of course, I could have easily asked each member individually for this same information, but the group forum combined with the assignment of physically writing down their thoughts encouraged discussion and brainstorming after each suggestion. It was an investment in their communication and critical-thinking skills, as well as an investment in the culture of open collaboration and in setting an expectation that reflection and iteration are important.

This example is just one to highlight the value of team meetings that don't suck. Here are a few other concrete suggestions to make sure yours never do:

- Enforce start and end times. This shows you respect both your time and your team's time, a critical building block in harboring trust.

- Ensure that you leave a few minutes at the beginning for casual topics and fun, such as a regular getting-to-know-you question, weekend plans, and personal life updates. This is an important investment in culture and creates the social cohesion amongst your team that builds the trust they need to work well together.

- Engage every person, every time. This is critical for developing public-speaking skills amongst your team members. Not only does this ensure that the ideas of introverts are heard and shared, but it also shows that you expect your team to collaborate and work together to problem solve.

- Consider bringing in guest speakers regularly to share updates from other parts of the business. This gives you an opportunity to show off your team to other departments, as well as show your team that you want them to grow and learn about other parts of the company outside of the job right in front of them.

If your team does collaborate regularly or rely on each other for mission-critical projects, your team meetings should be more frequent and generally be more focused on content related to your team's ongoing projects.

I've seen some teams do a weekly (or even daily!) stand-up—where each person reports on what they're working on and what they need from each other—with lots of success. If you go this route, make sure you're also carving out time for the career-oriented conversations, guest speakers, company updates, etc. to encourage and enable culture and growth on your team in addition to just getting the work done. Perhaps these do not need to occur quite as frequently, but make sure they exist.

Get yourself off to a great start by engineering a productive, engaging way for your team to come together regularly.

Some takeaways for your team meetings regardless of your industry: Make sure your team has the space and respect to truly feel heard, the opportunity to practice speaking, and the chance to hear what you're working on and what the company priorities are. Remember that team meetings are a useful tool in setting a tone for what you expect in the workplace, like showing up, being present, and contributing enthusiastically. These building blocks will be important as you develop your team and personal career as a leader.

GIVING AND RECEIVING FEEDBACK

"Even your most talented employees have room for growth in some area, and you're doing your employee a disservice if the sum of your review is: 'You're great!' No matter how talented the employee, think of ways he could grow towards the position he might want to hold two, five, or 10 years down the line."
—Kathryn Minshew, Co-Founder of The Muse

To be the effective coach that your team needs, you're going to have to give up the illusion that being liked is the same as being respected.

Think back to a time when you received extremely tough feedback from a manager. I'm not talking about cruel or off-the-wall stuff. I'm talking about something that you didn't want to hear but needed to hear.

For me, this was my very first job, when my then-manager told me that I was coming across to my customers as being very immature and they weren't taking me seriously.

Ouch.

In the moment, it felt like I was being hit with a dagger. I think I cried myself to sleep that night. But years later, I am so grateful this manager told me what I truly needed to hear I credit a lot of my success to hearing those words, because they forced me to adjust my approach.

By the time you move into a management role, it's likely you'll already be familiar and, at least, somewhat comfortable with the concept of professional feedback. Well, buckle up. Feedback is now going to be a big part of your job moving forward. It's something you'll want to keep getting better and better at, so make sure you at least have some sort of feedback on your feedback from either your current manager or anyone you've given feedback to recently to get a sense of where you stand today going into this new chapter.

For better or worse, feedback is going to be one of the most important aspects of building trusting relationships with your new team and providing ways you can grow as a new manager. There's a lot of literature out there on how to effectively give feedback, so I won't start from scratch for this section, but I will give you some useful lessons I've gathered throughout my management career.

Let's start by discussing the feedback everyone likes to hear—positive feedback! It's equally important, if not more, to give positive feedback regularly and meaningfully, because it can even be more effective than critical feedback at creating the types of behaviors and habits you want for your crew.

This may seem counterintuitive, but I've had a lot of luck praising to high heavens the accomplishments and good habits of my team rather than nit-picking on mistakes. I generally find that positive reinforcement coupled with direct, meaningful, and compassionate corrections of mistakes causes better outcomes. As it turns out, the science of positive reinforcement validates this observation:

In an article for Entrepreneur magazine, Heather Huhman describes how negative reinforcement can cause "attrition because employees feel that their boss doesn't trust them." Jeff Miller, the senior director of talent management at Cornerstone OnDemand, a talent-management solutions company in Santa Monica, California, tells Huhman: "Positive reinforcement directly rewards the behaviors you want to see continue and/or expanded (…) This underscores the importance of knowing what behaviors you want to see you employees engage in." [13]

---

13 Heather R. Huhman, "It's Science, Baby! Proving the Power of Positive Reinforcement at Work," Entrepreneur, October 16,, 2017, https://www.entrepreneur.com/article/302489.

Did half of your crew get their project done on time? Name them all one-by-one in front of the group to create that warm respect and to showcase how you'd like it to be done.

Did your team member take on a new and interesting initiative on their own? Praise them in a one-on-one over a fancy coffee and nerd out together about how cool their new endeavor is.

To summarize, here are some tips for jazzing up your team's spirit with meaningful positive feedback:

- Deliver detailed and personalized feedback praising wins, even the small ones, right when they occur or soon after.

- Meet each person where they're at; resist the temptation to compare your team members to each other, and recognize when a personal win is a personal win.

- Tie the right kind of behavior to career and personal goals; rather than just saying, "Good job," say something like, "That great product demo you did for our new sales team helped legitimize your skills as an internal expert, which could position you towards your goal of getting a product role!"

Positive feedback works.

But if positive feedback is like the carrot approach, what about the stick?

How do you tell someone they're missing expectations or, even worse, performing in a way that causes a breach of trust? It's certainly not fun for either of you, but it is a part of your job that you'll need to embrace. Before we explore giving critical feedback where the miss is so severe that you would rather rub fire ants in your eyeballs than deal with these transgressions, let's back up for a moment.

Critical feedback is tough and requires emotional labor from the giver and the receiver to transact. Each person on your team deserves this courtesy and work from you.

Why?

Of all the ways in which your leadership benefits your team, your honest, compassionate, and actionable constructive feedback is one of the most important, if not the most important. Delivering this feedback demonstrates your investment in your team's success and shows that you are willing to do the hard—at times yucky—work for their benefit. The relative discomfort that it requires to do this effectively is well worth the effort.

So, you should embrace this responsibility and demonstrate to your team that you have a deep professional respect for them. Winning!

One important aspect of feedback you'll want to start thinking about is unconscious bias in your delivery of feedback, and coming to terms with the fact that any advice, guidance, or criticism you are giving your team is coming from a biased perspective, because literally all humans are biased. [14] I recommend doing some research into how to attempt to unwind some of the programming you've received in your life so you can untangle your inherent biases from the real, actionable, humane, and direct feedback you'll want to give your team.

It turns out that there's a lot of literature about gendered discrimination in the workplace, for example. [15] In performance reviews, certain terms

---

14   Take Harvard's "Implicit Association Test" here: https://implicit.harvard.edu/implicit/takeatest.html.

15   John Gramlich, "10 Things We Learned About Gender Issues in the U.S. in 2017," Pew Research, December 28, 2017, https://www.pewresearch.org/fact-tank/2017/12/28/10-things-we-learned-about-gender-issues-in-the-u-s-in-2017/.

magically appear in female evaluations versus male; this is especially clear in feedback that is qualitative, rather than quantitative. [16]

As just one example, Stanford University's Clayman Institute for Gender Research found the following: Common words in performance reviews for women include abrasive, emotional, and bossy. These words rarely occur in documented performance reviews for men. [17]

For feedback of this nature, ask yourself, Would I give this same feedback to someone outside of this demographic who had similar work performance? Would you tell your male team members they were unapproachable or came off as "ditsy?" Would you tell your female team members they were "killers" and "rock stars?" While you certainly don't want to tiptoe around tough conversations, it is important to make sure your feedback is neutral and that you would truly say the same thing about anybody with that particular set of behaviors.

Now, you probably got promoted to management because you're seen as a pretty fair and balanced evaluator of situations, but that doesn't mean you shouldn't work to overcome any perceptions you may have about your male versus female team members that could affect how you treat them.

You will also have unconscious biases about other demographics that might affect the type of feedback you'll be inclined to give: Age, ethnicity, and sexual orientation are some of the heavy hitters. However, there's more subtle ones, like political affiliations, educational attainment, veteran status, and language spoken at home, that might affect how you perceive your team and how you deliver that feedback.

---

16   Paola Cecchi-Dimeglio, "How Gender Bias Corrupts Performance Reviews, and What to Do About It," Harvard Business Review, April 12, 2017, https://hbr.org/2017/04/how-gender-bias-corrupts-performance-reviews-and-what-to-do-about-it.

17   Rachel Emma Silverman, "Gender Bias at Work Turns Up in Feedback," the Wall Street Journal, updated September 30, 2015, https://www.wsj.com/articles/gender-bias-at-work-turns-up-in-feedback-1443600759.

Similarly, be careful not to assume what anybody on your team is trying to achieve by projecting your own career ambitions or background onto them. Don't assume your early 20-something employees are planning to go back to grad school. Don't assume your 30-something employees are more interested in parenting and home-buying. Don't assume your baby boomers aren't trying to achieve the next level of their professions with the ambition of a startup founder. Do you follow?

I recall a meeting I was in with several other managers, in a session to determine the salary increases across our teams with our allotted budget. A particular individual, let's call him Derek, was being considered for a promotion. In discussing Derek's performance and aptitude for the upcoming period, it became uncomfortably clear that his age was an influencing factor, perhaps subconsciously and in coded language.

"Derek can't get a senior position—he's only been out of college two years."

"I was 10 years more experienced than he is by the time I had that salary."

Clearly, our leadership team was bringing a set of preconceived beliefs about age and competency into play when considering Derek's career path, as well as inserting their own expectations and career journey.

Don't do this. It's wrong (and it potentially jeopardizes you and your company legally), but unfortunately, it's all too pervasive in corporate culture. As a new manager, you'll probably be exposed to this sort of thinking, and will be in a position to set a different tone in your circles.

Ultimately, I've found that the best way to give feedback is to be direct and compassionate and connect it to the career or life goals that your team has stated they want to achieve. For example, if they're trying to get promoted to management themselves, structure your feedback in a way that gives them specific pointers on what they should focus on to develop executive decision-making skills, take on more responsibility, and interact with more senior leaders at the company. Or say they want to start their own company someday. In this case, give them lots of feedback regarding task prioritization, time management, and business acumen. Or maybe they're simply looking for better work-life balance. In this case, give them feedback about developing better boundaries and managing competing priorities.

And do all of this with emphasizing that they are good people—otherwise you wouldn't have hired them or kept them on—and that you believe they are capable of doing amazing work. They will rise or fall to whatever expectation you have for them, so hold a high standard, keep your team accountable, and don't be afraid of uncomfortable conversations.

It takes emotional labor to deliver feedback, but doing it regularly and with intention shows your team you're invested in their growth.

Finally, I'd like to address the topic of having to have a very difficult conversation, such as addressing a Serious Fuck Up. One of my old bosses explained this to me as the difference between a *misdemeanor* and a *felony*, and I think that comparison is accurate. When you have a team member not meeting expectations over a sustained period or doing something so out-of-bounds that you have to draw a hard line, you'll need to really be strong and direct with your feedback.

These conversations usually go one of two ways: 1) either you see a strong change of mindset and action in the positive direction, 2) or the bad pattern gets worse and ends in termination or separation. It's not fun, but sometimes these things happen, and you'll need to be decisive when that time comes.

Remember: Your whole team is depending on you to make fair decisions on behalf of all of them, and sometimes that means separating someone who isn't a fit or who is setting the bar too low for the performance you expect from your team.

You've got this!

THE SHIT UMBRELLA (THE BUCK STOPS WITH YOU)

"If your issues are with me, then deal with me. This has nothing to do with my ship, nothing to do with the Federation!"
—Captain Jean-Luc Picard [18]

I learned some of my best leadership tips from Captain Picard and Captain Janeway. You may laugh (I hope you do!), but fictional characters can be wonderful resources to draw inspiration from as you build your personal approach to leadership.

Experienced customer support people manager Emily Vermeulen describes her management style as a *shit umbrella*. I've always loved this metaphor

---

18   Star Trek: Nemesis, dir. Stuart Baird, 2002, Paramount Pictures, 116 mins.

and found it an apt way to describe the sudden, and often jarring, responsibility of being on the front lines of any and all escalations that affect your department.

Escalations are tricky. To maintain credibility with your customers, peers, and your company, you'll need to respond, manage, and ultimately de-escalate them, but it is tough to balance what has been described as the Urgent with the Important aspects of your job. These types of escalations span the gamut from client issues to project delays to, my least favorite, personnel escalations—that is to say, concerns raised to you about someone reporting directly to you.

While a personnel escalation doesn't quite fit the visual of the shit umbrella, it is another example of a type of quasi-emergency you need to deal with immediately and without obvious disruption to the business. Angry clients are always more pleasant to deal with than receiving a complaint about an inappropriate behavior from one of your team members.

What these escalation types have in common is that they're now a huge part of your job, so you'll need to learn how to find your inner zen…or at least fake it! Your success in this new phase of your career will be determined by your ability to embrace and even lean into the discomfort that comes from knowing that escalations can be unpredictable and unrelenting.

You may think of this as the new normal.

At first, escalations of all types will probably be an unsettling jolt of stress when you start managing a team, but you'll soon find your stride as you gain experience in your new role.

Here are a few methodologies you can use to deal with the inevitable escalations that will come across your desk over the years:

1. Whatever the nature of the escalation, respond to the person who raised it to you within at least one business day, even if you don't plan on taking action right away or don't yet know what the course of action is. **Respond calmly and gather as much information as you need to better understand the nature of the escalation.** Don't worry about questions that may seem silly—it's better to fully understand the situation, and asking provocative questions may actually help in impressing your counterparts. Be clear about what you intend to do as a next step by saying something like, "I'll review with my team and will get back to you tomorrow by noon," and make sure to follow through—your credibility depends on it! Also, consider the source of the escalation and the weight they carry. Is the source a manager lateral to you? An individual contributor bypassing their management chain and going directly to you? Your own manager escalating a situation directly? It will take some time to calibrate these different sources of escalations, but it is a factor that you should pay attention to.

2. If the escalation involves an unhappy customer, you might want to consider offering to talk to them directly or otherwise be put in direct contact with the customer. **This is when your new fancy manager title might give you some automatic advantages:** Sometimes a customer just wants to talk to somebody with the manager title, so they feel heard and acknowledged. Chances are, you've had some experience in situations like this before, so you already have some customer savviness to you. You might be surprised at how a customer responds to a title that communicates authority!

3. **If the escalation involves a complaint about someone who reports to you, you'll want to really do your due diligence here.** Of course, the escalation happened for a reason, so you should process the data point with appropriate urgency and thoughtfulness. You'll also want to make sure you understand the full context of the feedback, especially as you are learning how to navigate your new reporting relationship

with the team member in question, and balance that data point with a 360-degree view of how they're performing. Understand that the underlying situation at hand needs to be addressed, and ultimately you are responsible for addressing any short-term issue to resolution that involves your team. If your team member dropped the ball, well, you are now ultimately responsible for picking it back up. Remember that the buck stops with you, and you need to lean in and drive the resolution.

Surprise! Managing escalations is your new normal. You'll get used to it.

Managing escalations is a combination of an art and a science and is something you'll get better at with time. Know that you'll never reach a zero-escalation state and embrace the fact that this will be an ongoing part of your new role. You're the boss now, so get ready to be that beautiful shit umbrella and spread yourself wide!

chapter 5

THE PERFORMANCE REVIEW OF A LIFETIME

"I liked challenging people and making them uncomfortable. That's what leads to introspection and that's what leads to improvement. You could say I dared people to be their best selves."
—Kobe Bryant, *The Mamba Mentality*

Do you fear public speaking worse than death?

If so, you wouldn't be alone. It's no secret that many people fear public speaking. In fact, it's one of the most pervasive phobias people have. [19]

But for managers like us, there's another fear lurking in our minds: the oh-so-dreaded performance review. Seriously. That's why this chapter is dedicated to showing you how to give a baller performance review.

---

19 Theo Tsaousides, "Why Are We So Scared of Public Speaking?" Psychology Today, November 27, 2017, https://www.psychologytoday.com/us/blog/smashing-the-brainblocks/201711/why-are-we-scared-public-speaking.

Now that you're on this side of the performance review, it's critical that you do this well to earn the respect of your team and empower them to move towards their goals. It is a fundamental part of developing your team members' abilities and attitudes, keeping them engaged in their work, and maintaining their loyalty to your company. Trust me, when your team feels—really feels—that you're invested in their growth, they will move mountains to deliver on expectations.

Usually, you'll be expected to deliver a formal performance review for your direct reports once or twice a year. While those meetings certainly should not be the only time you and your team members discuss performance, career goals, feedback, and opportunities, they should feel like more focused and formal discussions of these topics.

Pro tip: Absolutely nothing should feel like a huge surprise during a review if you're doing feedback correctly and regularly.

Also, performance review season is usually when you'll have an opportunity to offer promotions and raises, so get excited for those conversations! But—there's always a but—you must prepare yourself for some tougher conversations as well. Know that you may have to deliver some disappointing news about the lack of a salary increase or put in more formal terms your concerns about their ability to meet the expectations of the role.

Either way, performance review season is where you'll be doing some of the hardest and most thankless work of your management career, and as always, self-care should remain a top priority.

So, get your sleep, eat well, spend time recharging with friends and family, and do all the things that keep you grounded for this challenging and rewarding period of time.

Don't sleep on your performance review responsibilities. This is the right time to kick ass and take names as a people manager.

GATHERING PEER FEEDBACK, BUT NOT PEER PRESSURE

"Continuous improvement is better than delayed perfection."
—Unknown

When it comes to performance reviews, it's not time to wing it. Instead, it's time to prepare.

Recently, I interviewed an experienced people manager for my podcast, manager.flow, and asked him about his worst experience on the receiving end of a performance review. [20] He described what was pretty much a nightmare scenario.

His boss showed up late, appeared distracted, checked their phone constantly, and seemed to simply read off a laundry list of what felt like com-

20   You can find my Podcast Podcast Title at: [link]

plaints and nitpicks. Many of the complaints seemed to only encapsulate a situation from the couple of weeks right before the actual review and did not take into account the entire year of work leading up to the review.

Despite the job itself otherwise having been pleasant and exciting, the abject failure of this person's manager to put even an iota of effort into a thoughtful, constructive, and personalized review caused him to immediately start looking for other jobs.

Don't be that guy's manager.

So, what should you do?

A month or so before your reviews, you should solicit peer and leadership feedback from colleagues and, if applicable, any customers and/or partners that your various direct reports have worked with over the period of time in question.

There's not much more to it than this, but of course this is just the first step. I've heard many cases of managers basically stopping here at this point, delivering the feedback to the team member by reading out loud, verbatim, the feedback and comments from their peers without synthesizing it into broader concepts or areas of opportunity.

"So and so complained about the tone of an email you sent last week. And so and so thought your presentation to the client was unprofessional. So, there's your performance review! Good luck!"

Ummm...nope. Just...nope.

You aren't going to do this, of course. Gathering and digesting peer and leadership feedback is a technical step to your performance review process, but it's not the end of it.

Remember, feedback is useful to the degree that it's one person's perception of your team member's performance. Your job is to coalesce these data points into an overall narrative about wins and areas of opportunity with respect to your expectations, their career goals, and their effectiveness in achieving milestones towards both.

In soliciting feedback from the peers of my team members, I will often explicitly encourage them to not sugar coat or share information with the same tact as they would use directly with the person. It's my job to do that as an overall conversation with my team member. Reinforcing that with the request for peer feedback is helpful, so they don't worry about saying anything that will be repeated verbatim to their peers and potentially strain the relationship.

Here are some prompts that work well for soliciting thoughtful feedback, along with a request to send over examples if they're able to recall them.

- What are some of the highlights of working with Sean?

- What were some ways Sean has influenced the business for the better last year?

- Can you describe some challenges you've experienced in communicating with Sean?

- What are some things that could be holding Sean back from hitting their career goals?

Finally, if your team members are a part of customer- or partner-facing operations, it's important to solicit direct feedback from them. You may have a harder time getting an honest answer here, because customers are often reluctant to deliver critical complaints about people as opposed to the product itself.

Following is a sample template that I've used to reach out to customer contacts to get a sense of how they perceive the work of my team members. You can use it and build from it for your own specific case.

Good morning, Linda –

My name is Emily Tsitrian and I lead the implementation team at Mustang Inc. In the spirit of continually trying to strive to better service our customers and ensure we are delivering the highest quality of service possible, I wanted to reach out to solicit direct feedback about your experience with Sean Adelson.

We would like to understand how your experience with our process, team, and implementation was compared to that of other software implementations you have been through.

To be direct, what were the strengths of Sean, and what were areas of improvement?

If a phone call is a better format for you to share your thoughts, happy to set that up as well. Please send me 2–3 available times in the next week or two and we'll make something work.

—Emily

Store this feedback in a secure, confidential folder that's easily accessible but 100 percent locked—ideally in the same place you store any unsolicited feedback you may receive outside of the performance review period. Return to these notes later, when you're constructing the main themes and overall narrative of the performance review.

THE (WO)MAN IN THE MIRROR

"The journey into self-love and self-acceptance must begin with self-examination...until you take the journey of self-reflection, it is almost impossible to grow or learn in life."
—*Iyanla Vanzant*[21]

The most telling part of your team members' self-awareness and hunger for an investment of your coaching is the effort they put into the self-reflection portion of their performance review.

Usually, a company will deliver a canned set of prompting questions to all employees about six weeks before the scheduled performance review period and set a pre-established target date for their completion. These questions and their answers are generally distributed via internal HR software.

It's disappointing, but also revealing, when a team member responds to the prompts in one or two sentences. For example, I recently read a self-reflection that essentially said, "I want to get better at project management and also make more money."

In my experience, how seriously your team members take this process will vary widely. For the people keen on rapid professional advancement, these self-reviews might include a long list of accomplishments over the previous period as well as a firm and clear vision of their desired next step. If so, great!

This will make your job easier if you choose to advocate for them around review time to receive promotions and raises. If your other team members don't provide a thorough self-review, you'll have to do more of the

---

21   Iyanla Vanzant, *Until Today! Daily Devotions for Spiritual Growth and Peace of Mind* (New York, NY: Atria Books, 2012), 13.

heavy lifting to gather similar data for them, and inevitably you won't do as great of a job as they would since, well, they're much closer to the work than you are.

For that reason, you should always encourage your team to frequently note or save an ongoing list of accomplishments outside of the performance review cycle. (By the way, you should do the same.) Don't hold their hand through this. It really should be on them to remember to do, but some regular reminders will reinforce that you are invested in their professional progress and want to work with them to help them succeed.

After your team members submit their self-reflections, you'll integrate their perspectives on their work and goals with the overall review. Make sure you read it thoroughly and write down both your initial reactions to it as well as the one-layer-deeper questions you have about their thoughts.

HOW THE ~~SAUSAGE~~ SEITAN GETS MADE

"We haven't discussed the subject of payment.…"
—Ursula [22]

Ahhh, the subject of payment. Everyone's favorite.

Now you'll be making a series of micro decisions within a given frame-work to determine how much you will pay your employees for the upcoming period.

But before we get into the nitty-gritty, be aware that front-line managers typically aren't in the position to set an overall budget for their department, including salary tiers for the roles in their team. The overall budget is set by

---

22   "Poor Unfortunate Souls," from The Little Mermaid, dir. Ron Clements and John Musker, Walt Disney Pictures, 1989, 83 mins.

a combination of finance, HR and execs, and then trickles down to front-line managers, who are restricted to a set of inputs when determining pay and bonuses.

Your leadership team is putting an enormous amount of trust in you to make those decisions fairly and equitably, which is honestly a huge statement!

Being on this side of the pay negotiations is both thrilling and stressful, and you've got a lot of things to consider. These days, people discuss salary and compensation much more openly (and rightfully so—pay inequity thrives on secrecy), so you will need to have a lot of justification for the allocations you're about to make. For example, you certainly don't want to be in a situation where your female team managers' average salary is meaningfully less than the average salary pulled in by your male team members with no other clear differentials in experience, contributions, or tenure.

Typically, compensation decisions happen in tandem with the review process, so as a part of the seasonal review cycle, you'll be expected to make a recommendation to your leadership team for how to divvy up a spread of cash across your team. From there, your own manager will review these recommendations with you and provide input. These then will normally go over to your HR or compensation team for final approval.

It will probably go like this:

1. Your finance department issues an overall budget for raises, merit increases, and promotions for your entire department.

2. From the budget, you make some recommendations in increases across the spread of your team.

3. You justify your recommendations by meeting with your own manager and explaining your thinking.

4. Your manager and you will refine and iterate on these recommendations after lengthy discussion and debate.

5. Your manager then sends these recommendations over to their head of department, who will review, adjust, and send to HR.

6. HR and/or finance makes the final determination, which is sent to you a few days before the scheduled performance review.

7. You deliver the information personally about any adjustments to compensation during the performance review, and document in some central HR software that the information has been delivered.

8. You may also be responsible for emailing some official paperwork or document containing this same information after the review has occurred.

These steps must be followed sequentially and with precision, because you are covering a lot of ground in a short period of time. You need to ensure that you have ample time to add context to any changes in compensation prior to when your team members see the bump in their paychecks.

Of course, some of this context will feel good, but some of it won't, depending on their performance over the prior period. So, on top of preparing the actual content of the review, you'll need to start matching that content to a message about salary adjustments and/or bonuses that you'll be offering.

The moment you realize you're responsible for determining people's raises.

Determining salary adjustments during performance review season can feel scary at first, but you'll get the hang of it.

You might be wondering what happens if your team members take the opportunity to negotiate their salary during their performance review? It is likely to happen, and you should be prepared to handle this conversation.

If this does occur, write down exactly what was discussed and notify your manager immediately that this conversation has taken place. From there, you will need to quickly mobilize your HR, finance, and leadership team to evaluate if there is in fact any wiggle room and whether this negotiated increase would be available. Typically, the salary decisions made in advance of performance reviews are final, so you won't have much, if any, flexibility to offer any more.

The uncomfortable truth (that your team members won't readily realize) is that you have very little actual control over these sorts of decisions, and it is exceptionally rare that an upward adjustment is possible after the entire process has been completed. It will usually be a judgement call made unilaterally by your boss or your boss's boss in coordination with HR and finance. It can be done, but it is a lot of operational hassle and is only worth pursuing if you feel very strongly and are willing to stick your neck out there to justify the change. If this is the case, it doesn't reflect well on you that you didn't argue for that particular person's raise in the first place when the initial budgeted spread was available. So, while you may feel tempted to raise hell on behalf of your team member to advocate for a raise, it could actually backfire and make you look like an amateur for not having recommended such a raise in the first place, so be careful when managing this situation.

For that reason, you should be very deliberate and have ample justification for your initial set of recommendations, and be 110 percent prepared to explain the rationale behind the outcomes and in your delivery of the information to your team member. If you've done your job well prior to the performance review session, your team members will have a clear understanding of whether they're meeting and/or exceeding expectations for their role, so nothing will be outrightly surprising. If it is, and your team members seem caught off guard by what they perceive as an unfair compensation adjustment, you need to think about how well you've done in anticipation of the review in helping them understand feedback on their performance.

Sigh. I know it's a lot, and it's not easy. The bottom line: As part of your performance review responsibilities, you'll likely be determining compensation adjustments. Here are a few things to keep in mind as you proceed:

- You'll need a **clear head and a couple undistracted hours** to make your first pass at submitting salary adjustment recommendations.

- Take **copious notes about your thought process** as you do; these will be invaluable when you run your recommendation by your leadership team.

- **Expect about a two-week turnaround from your leadership team and HR** teams to finalize compensation decisions after you submit yours.

- **Schedule your employee reviews when you're sure of the exact window** between when these will be finalized and before they would see the adjustment in their paychecks.

THROW THE CAREER LADDER OUT THE WINDOW

"There's just some magic in truth and honesty and openness."
—Frank Ocean [23]

As they say in show biz, it's time to break a leg.

The final preparations and delivery of your performance reviews is your time to show the fuck up, perhaps more than you ever have before, as a first-time people manager. This is the moment for you to deliver all the value you can to your team members, set expectations for the upcoming period, cover your ass (in an HR sense) if there are future performance issues, and remind your employees why they want to work for you.

At this point, you should've read their self-reflections, mulled over peer feedback, made some determinations about salary changes, and collected a good idea of what you want to say. But before we get into the actual delivery of the review, it's important to formulate your talking points in a larger conceptual framework.

Now, here's where you really are going to shine in these review sessions.

Any manager worth their salt can deliver feedback as a simple regurgitation of peer feedback and set goals with their team members. But what separates

---

23   Amy Wallace, "Frank Ocean: On Channel Orange, Meeting Odd Future, and His Tumblr Letter," GQ, November 20, 2012, https://www.gq.com/story/frank-ocean-interview-gq-december-2012.

the good manager from the great one is making the effort to prepare and provide a holistic performance review that takes into account the entire set of circumstances team members are experiencing.

Ultimately, the review helps the team contextualize their goals in the broader business and industry structure, providing honest and actionable feedback to that end, and leaves the person receiving the review feeling inspired, energized, and seen.

And here's where your value-add really matters. Industry knowledge and company context are concepts you will categorically understand given your higher level and relatively more thorough exposure to your space and leadership team. Connecting your own knowledge at your reporting level with their lived perspective is key to delivering a phenomenal performance review.

For example, say an aspiring team member of yours wants to work together to establish the best pathway to attain the elusive director of marketing title.

A good manager might sit down with their team member at review time and lay out a series of goals to get closer to this title, but a great manager will ask provocative questions and break down this stated goal in industry context that illuminates something like the following:

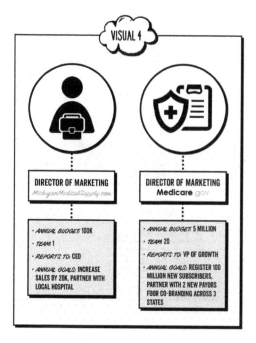

Clearly, achieving a promotion to director of marketing at MichiganMedical-Supply.com (a fictional company) and director of marketing for a behemoth like Medicare.gov will be a significantly different accomplishment.

Is your mind blown?

Well, get ready, because you're about to blow the lids off of your team members' stated career goals with this concept, which you can easily do by describing the example in the preceding chart.

The biggest takeaway is that the pursuit of a simple job title or a single promotion is myopic and, ultimately, a low-value experience if focused on solely in a performance review.

So, let's take things much deeper.

First, we need to see what not to do. Let's unpack what a traditional career ladder looks like.

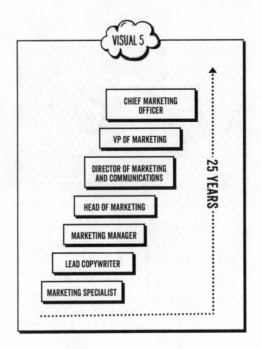

Old-school career ladders focus primarily on moving up as quickly as possible into new titles. But this falls too short. Compare this chart with the previous one—not all matching job titles are equivalent across industries and companies.

As illustrated in the chart comparing the responsibility and scope of a director of marketing for a hypothetical company, MichiganMedicalSupply. com, versus Medicare.gov illuminates a world of difference between these two titles, even within a similar industry.

So, for example, if someone on your team says they want to be a director of marketing and asks you for help in getting there, this is your signal that their thinking about their career trajectory needs some development.

And that's where you can deliver value.

Now, take a look at the career pyramid concept below, popularized by American billionaire and business executive Carol Bartz, one of my personal heroines of business and leadership.[24]

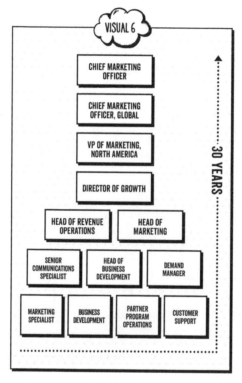

The career pyramid takes a little longer, but it's a much more stable career structure with a broad foundation across multiple disciplines. To achieve this result, lateral moves and cross-functional experience are key to gaining the type of expertise required to accelerate growth in the later stage.

Essentially, you're going to need to teach your employees, especially those at the beginning stages of their career, that playing the long game is key and the path to the job title of their dreams is not a straight line. It turns out that this occurs naturally on its own, as current data suggests that nowadays, people don't tend to stay in jobs for decades at a time. Typical

24   Stanford, "Carol Bartz: Pyramids, Not Ladders," YouTube video, August 13, 2008, https://www. youtube.com/watch?v=ZrvBuMXwmY4.

employees today stay at a job just over four years, and older employees typically have longer tenure than their younger counterparts.

Making lateral moves within companies, gaining meaningful experience across a variety of industries, and taking on new responsibilities outside your stated role are all power and money moves beneficial to building the foundation of a phenomenal career arc.

But you might be wondering at this point: okay, these charts are great, but how do we encourage upward growth within this framework? What do I encourage my team to focus on to build this foundation in their career to move them closer to their goals?

Drum roll, please. And if you haven't already, go put on your fancy pants for this next section.

Meet the influence and impact ladder.

In contrast to the simplified career ladder your team is used to referencing when visualizing growth, the influence and impact ladder helps illustrate the more tangible portion of what you can deliver to your team during their reviews.

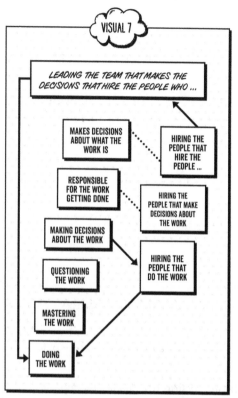

Rather than focusing on moving up the career ladder by playing the title game, focus on moving up the influence and impact ladder by upleveling yourself and assessing which rung you're on and what, realistically, will move you to the next rung.

In the career ladder progression depicted above, each rung represents not a promotion exactly, but an exponential, yet concrete, uplevel. In my experience, these uplevels almost always precede the traditional career upleveling depicted by the old-school career ladder.

To break it down, with any new role or entry into a new industry, people start at the bottom, **doing the work.** At this point, almost all focus and coaching should be oriented towards **mastery of the work.**

Once you have mastered the work, your focus and challenge is to **question the work**. To break it down further, I don't mean questioning as in literally "asking questions"—that's the easy part. The challenging part is the thought process that leads to critical and thoughtful reckoning about the different aspects of the work, innovating on how to do the work better, and looking for holes and inefficiencies that can be fixed.

For example, "Why are there so many emails from my customer?" is asking questions. "How can we better prepare our customers for self-sufficiency so we can scale more easily and give them back valuable time?" is questioning. See the difference?

If your team member is showing progress and achievement in **questioning the work**, you can start coaching them towards developing a key skill known as executive decision making and push them into opportunities where they'll be **making decisions about the work**.

Remember, each progression up this ladder represents a monumental upleveling of ability. It can take as much time, or even more, as the traditional ladder, which only describes an advancement in title. Moving into a role or even gaining an internal responsibility for making decisions about a workstream is huge!

Is your team member wearing their fancy pants yet? They should be. Because this is the point where their career growth potential starts to get really exciting and where you can work together with them to strategize about how to expand their impact and opportunities.

Now, the **making decisions** rung of the ladder also represents a decision point or branch from which someone can move laterally into a people-manager role or continue to move upward into higher and higher levels of responsibility as an individual contributor.

In fact, you've probably just moved over into this cohort yourself if you're reading this book!

For now, let's continue exploring upwards, following the individual contributor progression. It's likely that, as a first-time people manager, your team will be relatively junior in their tenure. That is, your team's levels on the impact and influence ladder will realistically be on one of the first three rungs, so it will be your job to help them see that if they don't.

No doubt, some of them will be clearly exhibiting some aptitude and maybe even behaviors that are higher up on the ladder, and that should be highlighted and encouraged! But to reach these upper echelons of impact and influence, you should push your team to fire on all cylinders to confidently move to the next rung.

Approaching the **responsible for the work getting done** tier, you'll start seeing people at the level in their career where they are prominent within an organization and industry and have broad swaths of influence. These generally correlate to a VP or senior director role on the traditional career ladder and are attainable without also specifically acquiring people-manager responsibilities. However, they are often peers of people managers in terms of organization structure.

By the time people are **making decisions about what the work is** or even nearing the top of the org chart, **leading the team that makes the decisions**, individuals are approaching C-suite roles. If you think about the role of senior executives, you'll realize that the actual work that they do has very little to do with the day-to-day operations itself.

But...are you ready for the fun part?

At each level, the cycle starts all over again! It's like Inception, but better, because it's real.

Or is it?

Just kidding. In all seriousness, this is where it gets really cool—the fact that the entire system can be replicated over and over and reapplied at each level.

For example, you are probably in the box of **hiring the people who do the work**, and you are also simultaneously in the box of **doing the work**. That is, you are **doing the work** of managing people. Have you mastered people management yet? Nope!

But don't feel bad! A first-time chief marketing officer (CMO) will also simply be **doing the work**, and yet simultaneously **making decisions about the work**. So, it's possible to be at different levels of the impact ladder for different aspects of your career. As a first-time manager, you might have achieved mastery when it comes to running a team meeting, but when it comes to giving feedback, you might be just **doing the work**.

At the end of the day, the impact and influence ladder wins every time, and is applicable across industries, roles, and stages of life. Your job is to help illuminate which rung your team members are on and give them practical and inspired directives to work towards the next rung. Focusing on moving up this ladder will inevitably move them up the traditional career ladder as well, but in a much more holistic and impact-driven way.

And so forth!

CURTAIN CALL!

"I get butterflies, for sure…I want so badly to be successful, so all that kind of comes out. But when you talk about butterflies and all that, it means you're prepared for the moment…that you want to be successful."
—Stephen Curry

By now, you've prepped for weeks and done the heavy lifting to prepare for your performance reviews, so it's almost time to show up and kick ass. But before you do, there's a few final logistics to work through to ensure you and your employees are set up to have an enjoyable, meaningful, and productive performance review.

I know, I know…more work?

Listen, you're almost there, but unless you ace the actual execution of the review, your hard work in prepping will be for naught! Time to bring your A game—as if you ever don't—and stay focused and grounded until the end of this period.

Chances are, your team members have been anxiously awaiting these reviews with a mixture of dread and excitement. Likely, it's not hard to empathize with since, until very recently, you were in the same position. It's not hyperbole to say that reviews can in fact be life changing and career altering. For better or for worse, they tend to remain either a highlight or lowlight of an entire chapter in someone's career, so this is not the time for you to half-ass it.

As discussed in the previous section, you'll want to schedule the actual review as a calendar hold with your team member shortly after receiving confirmation on pay and promotion changes from your HR partner, ensuring it occurs before the actual pay change is reflected in their paycheck.

You don't want your team members to find out about their pay changes through their paycheck before you've had a chance to message the reasons around any changes.

All that being said, you're almost officially ready for performance review season. Now we just need to go over my pro tips for performance reviews, along with a foolproof method for how to run a meeting.

To rock this last climactic portion of the review cycle, meet my pro tips:

1. Schedule the harder ones first and do not schedule more than two in one day to give yourself some breathing room.

2. Give yourself at least one day's break in between reviews, so that you can take some extra time to decompress between each one and mentally prep for the next ones.

3. Block 30 minutes or so after each review so you can complete any write-ups in the HR system of record while it's fresh in your mind.

4. Rehearse with a trusted management peer any difficult conversations you anticipate having and include two to three talking points for really difficult conversations. Ask your management peer to role-play how you think your employee may respond.

5. Meet in a neutral, physically comfortable place, if in person, such as a conference room or even offsite at a coffee shop or park bench. Ensure you are eye level with your employee and showing physical signs of being present and comfortable, such as a leg crossed comfortably over your knee. Turn off any notifications or distractions. You shouldn't be reachable during this time by anyone.

6. If your team member gets emotional, tell them to take a deep breath, and show concern for their emotional and physical well-being. Offer

to reschedule the remaining portion of the review once they've composed themselves. The truth is, your employee is no longer able to hear you once they've become visibly upset.

Finally, let's address the overall structure of the review. This is definitely one of the aspects of the review that you can stylize most to meet your own approach. Over time you will find a rhythm and flow that works for you.

Generally, I approach these meetings with the following five steps.

STAGE 1: BANTER

Me: "Good afternoon, Kelly, how are you doing today?"

Kelly: "Fine, but I'm a bit nervous. How are you?"

Me: "Totally normal to feel nervous. I'm usually a little nervous during my reviews also, but I always take it as a good sign because we care so much about our careers! The day we stop feeling nervous is the day we probably don't care that much anymore, and that's not a good thing. But thank you for telling me."

Kelly: "That makes sense. I just always get nervous this time of year."

Me: "I get that. Let me just start by saying how much I appreciate your investing time into this process, and how excited I am for your next six months and to watch your career grow over the rest of your life. I also appreciate being a part of this chapter and the trust you've given me to be your leader. I take that very seriously and, at the end of the day, we both want exactly the same thing, which is for you to succeed!"

Kelly: "That makes me feel so much better! I'm excited for the next stage, too."

STAGE 2: SELF-REFLECTION

Me: "Great! Let's get started by reviewing what you wrote in your self-reflection and your goals. I had a couple of clarifying questions about what you wrote, so when we get to those, I'll just pause, ask them, and take notes."

I then summarize the self-reflection, ask any clarifying questions, and affirm any notable accomplishments the employee stated. I will also be sure to add one or two of my own, to show the employee that I've been paying attention to their wins and to put them in a good headspace before some of the critical feedback.

Me: "Thanks again for such a thoughtful self-reflection. I always think that self-awareness and the ability to look back at one's accomplishments is so important to continued progress and career satisfaction. Now, I'd like to move on to summarizing some of the peer and customer feedback I received, which I think is useful in helping understand where you're already excelling and where there might be some opportunities to focus more in the upcoming year."

Kelly: "Sounds good!"

STAGE 3: PEERS

Me: "So, as you know, I spoke with a small number of your peers across the company, as well as the customers you've worked with this last year. Bottom line is—and this shouldn't surprise you—overall people love working with you and enjoy your positive energy and professionalism both internally and externally."

I will then attempt to quote one or two warm reviews verbatim.

Kelly: "Oh, that's awesome to hear! I am thrilled to hear people cited my professionalism this year, as that's been something I've been working hard on. I know I can come off as being too casual, so I have been really focusing on upleveling. Great to hear it's been noticed!"

Me: "It certainly has. That said, I think there's a couple things to focus on next to take this to the next level. I heard from a couple of people internally that they had a hard time processing your emails, which sometimes tended to be a bit long and not super polished. They also expressed some frustration in not having a clear picture of the status of your projects at times. Does it surprise you to hear that?"

Kelly: "Oh no, not at all. I get really overwhelmed with the amount of emails I get, and I put them off way too long."

Me: "That's a common challenge of people in this industry, but certainly one that you can overcome. The bad news is that, unfortunately, when these issues occur it paints a bad picture of your skills and can cause people to lose trust in your ability to finish the project. You and I know that's not true, so we need to work on bringing your email communications up to the standard that reflects your true abilities. That said, I have a few ideas and specific suggestions for getting better at this, which will ultimately save you time in the long run and get you closer to your goal of moving into a senior level role."

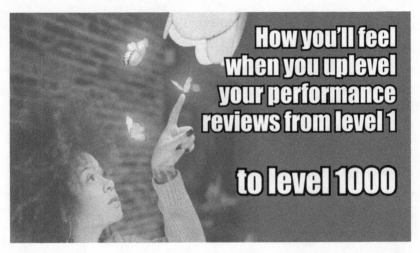

Level up your performance reviews and you'll reap the rewards for months.

STAGE 4: EXPECTATIONS

Kelly: "Do you mean to say I won't be getting this promotion right now?"

Me: "Correct. I know it doesn't feel good to hear that and that this is a huge goal of yours. But trust me when I say that I want this for you, too, and I think we can work together as a team to get you closer."

I will monitor Kelly's emotions and body language to see if he needs some additional time to process this bad news. I know he won't be receptive to my suggestions until he is.

Kelly: "I'm really disappointed, but do want to know what I can do to work towards this next time."

STAGE 5: NEXT STEPS

Me: "Understood. Let's then spend the rest of the review going through some actionable habits you can incorporate into your workday to achieve mastery of the role, which is definitely doable and a key component of achieving your goals."

I'll then share two to three actionable pieces of advice with the employee, but only ones I think they can realistically achieve in the upcoming period. I will also message any salary increases or bonuses they can expect in their next paycheck.

Me: "Okay, since we're getting close to the end, let's wrap things up. I do want to circle back to what I said at the beginning and very much meant: I so appreciate your work and effort and remain enthusiastic about the value you bring to the team. I know you're going to be wildly successful, and I look forward to working together to make it happen for you!"

Kelly: "Thank you. I can tell you put a lot of time into this, and I appreciate that."

Me: "Of course. I'll be putting a summary of this in your HR record in the next hour or two so you'll have it there, too, and you can expect to see the salary adjustment in the upcoming paycheck."

BRINGING IT ALL TOGETHER

Behold, the BSPEN Method. You can remember this as the "No BS" Method, even though the acronym clearly has BS in it. Just go with it and remember that BSPEN means banter, self-reflection, peers, expectations, and next steps. Got it?

The following steps provide a comprehensive timeline. These are your key steps to delivering the performance review of a lifetime:

1. **Six to eight weeks before**: Gather peer (and customer, if applicable) feedback from five to seven sources. Read and store each piece you

receive in a safe, secure folder. Set it aside after you read it and return to it later.

2. **Four to six weeks before**: Encourage your team to complete their self-reflections thoughtfully and thoroughly. Remind them that this is a great opportunity to list the accomplishments they feel most proud of and think about where they'd like to go next in their careers and lives.

3. **Three to four weeks before**: Using the inputs from peer and customer feedback and self-reflections (as well as your own judgement), make recommendations for promotions, raises, and bonuses alongside your manager and HR peers.

4. **Two to three weeks before:** Construct the narrative of the review, considering the impact and influence ladder and the stated goals of your employee, and prepare your messaging around what you antici-pate their salary, raise, promotion, etc. to be.

5. **Two weeks before**: As soon as you receive final confirmation from HR as to any salary, promotion, and bonus information, schedule your review with your team member with some time built-in before they will see the comp adjustments in their paycheck.

6. **One week before:** Do a final round of review or prep for your review, listing out talking points and, if needed, practice messaging with man-ager peers or your own manager if you anticipate any difficulty.

And finally, I want to address what you should do on the off chance that your performance review, or frankly any feedback session, goes awry (in other words, you believe someone is having a mental health crisis). You are absolutely not expected to be a therapist, nor are you trained to give qualified assessments of someone's mental health.

But, if there's clear indications that your team member needs expert help, it is a little fraught for you to suggest therapy or provide any sort of diagnosis. Try using a prepared approach such as, "It sounds like you're really struggling here, and I don't know how to help. Can I refer you to HR or another HR-provided resource to talk to a professional who can help you through this?"

All in all (mental health situations aside), performance reviews are a prime opportunity to shine in your new role. Provided you follow the steps and add the special element of your magic, you're going to an absolutely terrific job.

chapter 6

WHAT'S YOUR RELATIONSHIP FICO SCORE?

"I've learned that people will forget what you said, people will forget what you did, but people will never forget how you made them feel."
— Carl W. Buehner [25]

It's so true, and you know that. Otherwise, you wouldn't have cared enough about doing well as a manager to have purchased this book and made it all the way to chapter 6.

As a first-time manager, it will take some time to adjust to your new workload and how you use your time day-to-day. By now, you should have some sense of the tactical aspects of your new role and at least be able to function operationally in your position. But, of course, you don't just want to function, do you? You want to kick ass as a manager.

---

25   Richard L. Evans, Richard Evans' Quote Book (Lebanon Junction, KY: Publishers Press, 1971).

The secret sauce to working your way to kick-ass status is through your relationships with your team.

Your relationship with your team is like a credit score.

Let me be frank: You will struggle to be successful as a people manager without having a rock-solid foundation with the people on your team. This can be surprising coming from an individual contributor role, because the work there is more clearly defined.

Have you heard that adage that people leave managers, not jobs? Well, I'm sorry to say it, but there's a lot of truth in that!

Trust me—you don't want to be that manager whom the team gossips and complains about for being so aloof, out of touch, and so hyper focused on the execution of the work that team members are constantly plotting an exit strategy. And once they start leaving your team, you will be scrambling to backfill their work; this time suck will further deteriorate your already surface-level relationships with your remaining team. The resulting death spiral is probably something you've observed less-than-stellar managers struggle with.

The good news? You absolutely can avoid this trap by investing in your relationships with your team.

You might be surprised at how much effort and time this takes, but the reality is that developing, maintaining, and investing in a functional and productive relationship with each of your new direct reports is just as much your job as approving PTO.

The bad news? This area of your new role is the hardest one to give specific advice for because human relationships are pretty dang complicated. While I consider myself someone with a decently high emotional intelligence, human psychology is…messy…and an extensive field of study beyond most of our basic academic understanding.

Good news again, the bonus track: Intention and focus here is everything.

You won't get it right all the time, and that's okay!

You'll need to accept that. You also can't apply canned advice from a business book and expect that your employees will fawn all over you and sing your praises. Nope. You've got to develop your own style and methods, but if you bring your best intention and humility to each conversation, you will get there over time.

As you take inventory of all the relationships in your life, you'll realize there are some broad categories you've probably figured out how to navigate, while others are more of a struggle.

You know it. Relationships are hard work!

At the very least, you probably have some sort of a defined relationships with your parents, siblings, and friends (although these can vary widely depending on social norms, time of life, circumstances, etc.). You may also have romantic relationships, professional relationships, collegial relationships—the full gamut.

But this is where things get relevant.

If you've ever had a therapist or coach, you've gotten some experience in a relation that is emotionally oriented but set within predefined boundaries. Because you have a sense of these norms, you know that you wouldn't be friends with your therapist, wouldn't use your romantic partner as a business mentor (generally), and may not think of your parents or your children as people you can have extensive conversations with about your career interests and passions.

My point is that every relationship in your life is different and unique depending on the context, the emotional significance, and the social norms. And that's how it is supposed to be.

As Homo sapiens, we didn't evolve to be lone hunters. Whether we are introverts or extroverts, we thrive in interconnectedness and an ecosystem of different social relationships, where we specialize, divide, and conquer using our unique talents for the betterment of the tribe.

In the modern day, nobody gets all their needs met by any one person or any specific category of relationship. That's part of why life is a complicated web of interpersonal ties, but that's also what makes it beautiful and interesting!

At the foundation of your success as a manager is your trust with your team, so your self-awareness goes both ways. You'll need to develop trust in your direct reports, and more importantly, they'll need to develop trust in you. Like other relationships in your life, you'll be making deposits in a trust bank you'll invest in, withdraw from, and ultimately take with you as one of your greatest memories or regrets to the next chapter of your career.

Understand each person needs to be managed a little differently. Don't be overly concerned with management theory, academic psychology, or anything that's in this or any other business book. Each relationship will be unique and different, and you and your team members will be equal partners in setting intentions and investing in a great working relationship with you, their manager.

Have regular and ongoing dialogue about what kind of support each person needs at different times. Ultimately, you'll both get out what you put into it.

Snap out of it!

You can't manage everyone the same way. Humans are complex and unique—much harder to manage than the work itself.

When I first take on new team members, I like to spend a lot of time getting to know them as professionals and as individuals, since it's also helpful to identify some general trends with how they like to work.

I usually start this conversation by sending them several prompts like the following that we can either discuss live in a one-on-one or more generally over email:

1. What professional accomplishment are you most proud of, at Acme or otherwise?

2. What has been a trait of the best manager you've ever had?

3. What has been a habit or trait of the worst manager you've ever had?

4. What is a technical skill, nonspecific to Acme, that interests you (e.g., SQL, Excel, or Tableau)?

5. What is an area specific to our Acme's space or product that interests you?

6. What is a soft skill you want to develop further (e.g., public speaking, executive decision making, negotiation, or project management)?

7. What is your favorite part of your current job?

8. What makes you feel the most acknowledged and appreciated at work: salary, title, level, networking, public praise, etc.?

Managing human beings is much, much harder than managing work or projects. Each person has a unique and complex personality, and establishing trust will take time and effort by both parties.

In the next section, I'll explain some generalities you may find in leading employees in different age demographics. Keep in mind that these are very basic assessments based on personal experience and the collective wisdom of business leaders and demographers, and it's really important to not project any prior expectations onto your team based on your own life experience or something you read in a book.

However, contextualizing some of the general trends is useful as you try to imagine the life experience of someone on your team and how it may or may not be different than others. The empathy and shift in perspective to understand another's life journey is an important step in empathizing with your team members so you can work well together in your new role.

MILLENNIALS

"Is this real life?"
—David after Dentist, YouTube video [26]

Let's start with millennials, since I fit into this category myself. The data seems to suggest that we late 20- and 30-somethings represent the biggest percentage of the labor force today. Oh, and we ruin everything, from movie theatres to diamond rings, [27] are careless with our money, [28] and value feelings over facts. [29] Also, we are just as addicted to tech as our younger Generation Z counterparts, but we are as jaded and over it as our Generation X elders.

Do you feel personally attacked?! I do (I mention as I scroll haplessly through TikTok, wearing athleisure pants and a slightly off-kilter topknot, and trade stocks on Robinhood).

That's okay, of course, you know that we dang millennials have gotten a somewhat bad rap as the stereotypically hardest demographic to manage, and to be honest, there is some merit to that!

Millennials have basically turned traditional management theory on its head and have stumped business schools, Gen X and boomer hiring managers, and HR professionals alike. In fact, this entire book is somewhat a

---

26 "David After Dentist," YouTube video, January 30, 2009, https://www.youtube.com/watch?v=txqiwrbYGrs&t=0s.

27 Andrew Josuweit, "5 Industries Millennials Are 'Killing,'" Forbes, October 22, 2017, https://www.forbes.com/sites/andrewjosuweit/2017/10/22/5-industries-millennials-are-killing-and-why/?sh=77c0fa8644e4.

28 Liz Knueven, "A startup founder who spent 100 hours interviewing millennials found 3 hangups usually keep them from being good with money," Business Insider, February 23, 2020, https://www.businessinsider.com/personal-finance/millennials-good-with-money-mindset.

29 Karl Moore, "For Millennials, Thinking And Emotions Are Equals – More or Less," Forbes, June 26, 2017, https://www.forbes.com/sites/karlmoore/2017/06/26/for-millennials-thinking-and-emotions-are-equals-more-or-less/?sh=2e8caa8676f2.

response to the relative lack of quality literature on the market for wisdom on how millennials function (or don't function) in the workplace.

To understand some of the nuances related to managing millennials, it's important to consider the historical context surrounding the life experience of this group.

From about 1950 to 2000, the American economy steadily grew,[30] and it was common for young adults to settle into careers fairly early in life and stick with their employers.[31] Households often had one wage earner, employers provided pensions, and unions were common in blue-collar jobs.[32]

All of that has changed dramatically in the past 20 years as the middle class has shrunk[33] and health care and education costs have skyrocketed.[34] Birth rates have gone way down, and the age of first birth has increased.[35] As such, the concept of saving for retirement and living a comfortable middle-class lifestyle is a lot more nebulous than in previous generations; this certainly affects how millennials connect to their employers.

My theory is that since millennials generally postpone having families of their own and realize the reality of their economic situation, they seek a different kind of emotional connection and relationship to their employers and managers than previous generations.

---

30   Jordan Weissmann, "60 Years of American Economic History, Told in 1 graph," The Atlantic, August 23, 20212, https://www.theatlantic.com/business/archive/2012/08/60-years-of-american-economic-history-told-in-1-graph/261503/.

31   The Associated Press, "Here's Why Your Parents Stayed at the Same Job for 20 Years," Fortune, Mary 10, 2016, c

32   Elisabeth Jacobs and Jacob Hacker, "The Risign Instability of American Family Incomes, 1969-2004," Econimic Policy Institiute, May 28, 2008, https://www.epi.org/publication/bp213/.

33   "America's Shrinking Middle Class: A Close Look at Changes Within Metropolitan Areas," Pew Research Center, May 11, 2016, https://www.pewresearch.org/social-trends/2016/05/11/americas-shrinking-middle-class-a-close-look-at-changes-within-metropolitan-areas/.

34   Stephen Moore, "Why costs are soaring for education, health care,"The Heritage Foundation, June 6, 2014, https://www.heritage.org/health-care-reform/commentary/why-costs-are-soaring-education-health-care.

35   "US birth rate falls 4% to its lowest point ever," BBC News, May 6, 2021, https://www.bbc.com/news/world-us-canada-57003722.

For example, take the protest and walkouts at Google in 2018.[36] These historic displays of organized protest for corporate social responsibility, especially in the tech sector, are a testament to how much has changed and what today's workforce values in a company that employs millennials.

The broader conversation surrounding #MeToo and #BlackLivesMatter is all part of a shifting collective consciousness about the role of an employer today. As a manager with millennials on your team, this is something you'll want to deeply, truly internalize as you empathize with the moral sentiment of your employees and understand the broader socioeconomic context in which this generation came of age.

Millennials are also doing all sorts of things that are stumping demographers. They're waiting until their mid-30s to have children,[37] they're living with roommates longer,[38] not buying cars,[39] and not saving for retirement the way other generations have.[40] Basically, their behavioral preferences have totally confused economists, as they just don't seem to line up with expectations from previous generations.

I believe that there are some additional reasons why millennials have deeper emotional and social connections to their employers. If, for example, you don't have a spouse and kids for a solid decade into your career, your

36 Daisuke Wakabayashi, Erin Griffith, Amie Tsang and Kate Conger, "Google Walkout: Employees Stage Protest Over Handling of Sexual Harassment," the New York Times, November 1, 2018, https://www.nytimes.com/2018/11/01/technology/google-walkout-sexual-harassment.html.

37 Ashley Stahl, "New Study: Millennial Women Are Delaying Having Children Due To Their Careers," Forbes, May 1, 2020, https://www.forbes.com/sites/ashleystahl/2020/05/01/new-study-millennial-women-are-delaying-having-children-due-to-their-careers/?sh=2bf8b4a2276a.

38 Alexandra Talty, "Skyrocketing Number of Millennials Living With Housemates," Forbes, November 3, 2015, https://www.forbes.com/sites/alexandratalty/2015/11/03/skyrocketing-number-of-millennials-living-with-housemates/?sh=528ae1e37265.

39 Lance Eliot, "The reasons Why Millennials Aren't As Car Crazed As Baby Boomers, And How Self-Driving Cars Fit In," Forbes, August 4, 2019, https://www.forbes.com/sites/lanceeliot/2019/08/04/the-reasons-why-millennials-arent-as-car-crazed-as-baby-boomers-and-how-self-driving-cars-fit-in/?sh=5d0c527b63fc.

40 Kathleen Elkins, "The No. 1 Reason Millennials Are Struggling to Save for Retirement—and It's Not Debt," CNBC, September 25, 2019, https://www.cnbc.com/2019/09/25/the-no-1-reason-millennials-are-struggling-to-save-for-retirement.html.

social and emotional life is probably going to revolve around your workplace as you'll seek a deeper connectivity with your colleagues.

As a millennial manager, you may feel your lifestyle aligns with these trends, or you could be the complete opposite! Regardless of your own personal situation, the demographic data is something you should pay attention to, especially when receiving management advice from someone who hasn't managed millennials (successfully) before, like any mentors, older-generation managers, and name-dropped managing books. Many of these books are woefully out-of-date!

Use these pointers to effectively connect with, empathize with, and motivate your millennial employees:

- Have direct and regular conversations about their life values, practicing your listening skills and repeating back, "This is what I'm hearing. It is important to you, is that correct?"

- Ask for feedback on what you and your company could be doing better to create culture and align it with a moral and cultural compass.

- Make loads of introductions to people in your network to show you're invested in growing *their* own brand and network.

- Spend time volunteering and reflecting together on why giving back is important.

- Get them connected to employee resource groups.

- Give them a phone call out of the blue just to catch up.

- Take them out for coffee or a walk around the block to just enjoy each other's company.

These small moments add up to lasting relationships and a higher quality of work. Investing that time up front will pay off in dividends when you need to ask them to take on tough projects or stay late working on an urgent issue.

Sure, you can knock millennial stereotypes, but the reality is they're facing skyrocketing student loan and health-care costs, unlike previous generations.

Finally, this generation came of age in a largely post-9/11 world and has faced one of the toughest economic conditions of the past century: the 2008 recession followed by the 2020 COVID-19 pandemic.[41] In light of these challenges, this generation is proving to be one of the most enlightened, altruistic, and driven generations who will work incredibly hard for a leader they believe in and a company vision they embrace, so don't write off this generation because they have a reputation for being hard to manage.

Understand this is a new frontier for managers such as yourself and embrace the journey! Lean into your relationships with your millennial team members with perhaps a deeper emotional intention that you may expect the relationship requires. Spend some extra time facilitating social connect-

---

41   Michelle Fox, "The Covid pandemic is worse than 2008 crisis for a majority of Americans, study says," CNBC, updated December 1, 2020, https://www.cnbc.com/2020/11/10/pandemic-worse-than-2008-for-a-majority-of-americans-study-says.html.

edness in the workplace, and insist your company has a commitment to values that align with what's important to you and your team.

GEN X

"When you don't talk down to your audience, then they can grow with you."
—*Prince*[42]

Tina, one of the Gen Xers I managed a few years ago, had just walked onstage to give a slide presentation at our department kickoff meeting in a hotel in downtown San Francisco. She and I had rehearsed all her slides together, so I knew she knew the material inside and out and had the passion to deliver a punch to the team!

After the first slide, she froze. The excruciating silence and blank stare that followed made me realize she was having a panic attack, onstage. She spoke into the microphone, "I can't do this," and looked at me, her eyes seeming to beg for help.

The audience was unbelievably kind and cheered for her to go on despite her nerves. After about 30 seconds, I realized that, indeed, I had pushed her too hard. I got onstage, took the mic from her, and delivered the rest of the slides myself.

After the session, she burst into tears in the hallway. I hugged her and let her know it was alright, that I had pushed her too far out of her comfort zone and we would try again next year.

It was then that I realized that because of Tina's Gen X status and years of work experience, I assumed she had the confidence and ability to take the

---

42   "Prince PBS Interview with Tavis Smiley 2004," YouTube video, March 4, 2020, https://www.youtube.com/watch?v=lvS9W1hIU4A.

stage. I realized I had been so focused on my millennial employees that I took for granted Tina's equal need for coaching and encouragement.

#ManagerFail, big-time.

That said, let's take a more holistic look at Gen X (1965–1980). Crack open your Snapple, open up your bag of Bugles, and channel your favorite Dawson's Creek character for this section.

Ahhh, Gen Xers, the generation that got to share time on earth with Nirvana and Reaganomics, and blissfully came of age in the modern era but without the proliferation of social media, cell phones, and 24-hour cable news cycles.

Does it even get much better than that? Scientifically speaking, no.

Admittedly, my experience managing Gen Xers is probably the most varied depending on their life experiences and career choices, but I will say that I've really enjoyed every opportunity I've had to manage employees in this cohort.

They probably have two or three decades of work experience under their belts already, so by the time you become their manager, they'll have already developed a number of workplace habits as well as the grit required to wade through tough situations. Of course, you should never 100 percent assume this is the case, as I did with Tina!

There are some exceptions to this, of course, such as someone who may be entering the workplace after an extended leave, perhaps to raise children or for other reasons. Or maybe your Gen X team member served in the military or recently immigrated to the country and is making a career change, for example.

As with anyone in any category, always be careful not to make assumptions about where you think your Gen X employee might be in life or project onto them where you think they should be based on where you expect yourself to be at their age. This was my fatal mistake with Tina. I put her in a position where I mistakenly assumed she would succeed.

When it comes to managing someone in Gen X, it's extremely important to spend a lot of time really understanding and even unpacking their priorities and what they intend to get out of this chapter in their career. Then you can coach them specifically on what their goals are, rather than focusing on making them better generalists (as I often do with younger generations, to give them the best foundation possible for future specialization).

Honestly, Gen Xers are loyal, hardworking, and wise if you prove that you are dedicated to their success, and it may take some time to prove that! It's not their first rodeo, and you won't be their first manager (and likely not the last) with pie-in-the-sky aspirations, so you're going to have to walk the walk. Gen Xers can smell your BS from a mile away, so don't peddle it. Instead, cut right to the chase.

They probably also have some very practical industry experience you should make a point to learn from. For example, if they started working in the 90s and were in any way connected to the dot-com bubble, they've certainly seen their fair share of economic ups and downs, and those insights are useful in interpreting the current economic atmosphere.

Gen Xers have likely seen companies and trends come and go and have experienced some hubris from that time that they can teach you about. Probe them for what their experience was like during that time. Then work with them to connect it to their current role to extract insights together, and ask for a lot of professional feedback.

Likely, they're still youthful enough to empathize and connect with millennials and Gen Z, but are old enough to have learned quite a few lessons the hard way, which, if leveraged, can help your whole team and company improve.

With Gen X, chances are high that they have a more defined home life, and that may include children who are adults or teenagers. If you yourself are young, you may even be closer to their children in age! Of course, you may encounter this with boomers as well, but with Gen X it can feel slightly awkward when you first take the reins. You may assume your Gen X employee sees you as in the same category as their children, or you may feel uncomfortable taking a leadership role over someone who could be your parents' age.

My advice is to take those feelings, set them aside, and accept with humility that you have been chosen to lead your team. You have something of value to offer your team members because of your unique abilities and experience.

Leverage your Gen Xers' perspectives for your own benefit!

Don't be afraid to have direct conversations with your Gen X team members about what they're experiencing in this stage of life. If they have older kids, ask questions about what they're up to. Are they graduating? Going to college? Struggling to figure it all out? Whatever it is, keep an open mind and push yourself to find connectedness to their situation and story. This openness and dialogue will help you lead your team and connect with your Gen X employees.

You'll also want to be mindful of other responsibilities your Gen X employees will have outside of the workplace and respect those boundaries. While other generations may very well have those responsibilities, I've personally found that Gen Xers are a bit more entrenched in family routines and their community. They are also slightly more likely than millennials to be parents, based on demographics alone. So, to fully include your Gen Xers, make sure your after-hours events are well planned and within reasonable work hours, have some flexibility with working from home or time off for family duties, and be mindful of the amount of notice you give folks who may need to travel. It may be a bit more than what's needed with a millennial, but it's the price you pay for having a diverse team that is fully inclusive. In the long run, you'll work fewer hours if your team is thriving, so don't be afraid to put the time in to make it work.

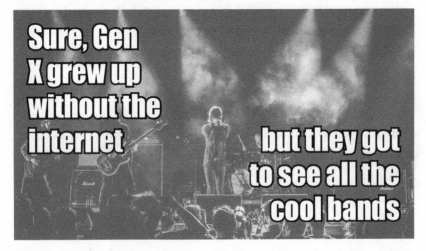

Gen X is the last cohort to really grow up without social media or the internet, but they still have a lot of pop culture touchpoints. Keep in mind they may be parents of adults or near-adults by now!

Finally, I recommend trying to find leadership roles for anyone on the team who is Gen X.

Even if it's not a future management role, encourage them to lead a project or own something strategic, and then coach them to ensure they're successful. Sometimes it can take a little more work to build up their confidence, but if you put this work in, the results will pay off greatly. Gen Xers have a unique combination of decades of work and life experience to offer your team along with having a modern perspective, and as a result, they can offer a gold mine of knowledge and mentorship in a management role.

Because of this, your team probably has some built-in respect for anyone in the Gen X category already, so nurture this and coach them behind the scenes to take on a leadership role. The returns will be massive from this investment, trust me on that.

To summarize, some of my best advice for managing Gen Xers is as follows:

- Dig into their experience in any industry, and make it clear you would love to learn from their career experiences outside of the current role.

- If they have family responsibilities, make it clear you respect those boundaries and that you can be flexible with when and how they work.

- Do not assume they don't need coaching or support just because they're more seasoned than younger cohorts.

- If they are interested in leadership roles, encourage this!

- Conversely, if they *aren't* interested in leadership roles, accept this, too! They may be in more of a lifestyle phase of their career where they simply have other priorities than career advancement.

- Have fun with them—your Gen X team members will be as loyal as hell and lifelong friends once you've earned their respect as a no-nonsense leader who actually cares.

BOOMERS

"Ah, but I was so much older then /
I'm younger than that now"
—Bob Dylan[43]

If you get the chance to manage someone in the baby boomer generation (1946–1964), consider yourself lucky. The generation that was born in the years after WWII has truly seen and experienced a lot and has so much to offer any workplace. Furthermore, the reality is that they're hitting retirement age soon, and the opportunity to have them on your staff will diminish as the years go by. If you find yourself in a situation where you have a team member in this demographic group, embrace the moment. Baby boomers have learned a lot of life lessons the hard way, and that can benefit you and your workplace. Approach this managing relationship with grace, curiosity, and most of all, respect.

Baby boomers, categorically speaking, came of age during the 1950s and 1960s, when the working world was a hugely different place.

To illuminate further, the economy was growing and stable, and the middle class was structurally gaining wealth and economic power with the rise of manufacturing and the early telecom giants. At that time, it was common to choose a profession at a young age and stay with that same employer over a lifetime, retiring into a healthy pension and relative economic comfort. Women were still relatively scarce in the workforce,[44] and many professional environments were likely racially homogenous.[45] Until the late 1960s when the pace of social and political change rapidly in-

---

43 "My Back Pages," written by Bob Dylan, 1964, 4 mins.
44 "Changes in women's labor force participation in the 20th century," U.S. Bureau of Labor Statistics, February 16, 2000, https://www.bls.gov/opub/ted/2000/feb/wk3/art03.htm.
45 Susan Hauser, "The Dream, the Reality: Civil Rights in the '60s and Today," Workforce, Apryl 10, 2021, https://www.workforce.com/news/the-dream-the-reality-civil-rights-in-the-60s-and-today.

creased, the economic and professional situation was a quite different reality than today.

Of course, much has happened between then and now, including the inflation of the 1970s, Reaganomics of the 1980s, the personal computing revolution of the 1990s, and the realities of a post-9/11 world.

The best part about boomers? They've been here for all of it!

Game-changing innovations and progress have been made in each decade since they came of age, and it's likely your team members have taken some or all of it to heart. Generally speaking, baby boomers have a well-developed work ethic defined by hard work, dedication, integrity, and loyalty, and often model these in the workplace. If you model your team around these values, you're setting up your team and yourself for a tremendous career.

I recommend approaching these relationships from a place of respect even more than others. Invest a lot of time in active listening with your baby boomer staff, asking them questions about what's working and what's not working in the workplace, and make space for their honesty. It's likely you'll have the greatest age differential with baby boomers if you yourself are a millennial, so it may take a bit of work for you and your employee to find common ground.

Trust me, you will find it with time and patience.

A final note on managing baby boomers: Don't automatically assume that this generation is technologically challenged. I have personally found that to be a somewhat tired trope that is sometimes true but often not. More commonly, I have found that the challenges with bonding between generations and inclusivity have more to do with pop culture or an overreliance on current cultural norms for communication.

If you're lucky enough to manage a baby boomer, take their advice to heart and soak up all the career and personal advice you can. It's extremely valuable in today's workplace!

For example, your baby boomer team member may not be super comfortable texting you or using Slack or some other instant messenger as your primary means of communication. They may find it more challenging to feel included if you focus your team culture on going to trendy restaurants, using viral memes, or speaking with a hashtag reference.

So, if you have baby boomers on your team, make sure your team culture and communication norms take that into consideration. Sometimes a good old-fashioned phone call will be the best way to connect with your new team member, and with time and patience, you'll find a happy medium to develop a bond and great working relationship.

To summarize, follow this advice for managing baby boomers:

- Get over your fear about phone calls and pick up the damn thing to call your baby boomer employees.

- As with Gen X, absorb all you can from your boomer employees' life and work experience. You don't have to emulate anything from the past, but knowledge is power and history repeats itself, so be insatiable about tapping into their knowledge!

- Do not talk down or be preachy to your boomer employees. This will alienate them and even offend them. You will need to earn their respect through your hard work and willingness to listen and grow first.

- Be direct and clear with your communications. Do not beat around the bush when delivering bad news.

GEN Z

> *"Age is foolish and forgetful when it underestimates youth."*
> —Albus Dumbledore, *Harry Potter and the Half-Blood Prince*[46]

Gen Zers are millennials on steroids.

I'm only half joking. Many of the generalizations that people make about millennials are also relevant to Gen Z (1997–2015), the generation coming into the workplace with their phones tethered to them, but bright eyed and driven to change the world.

Gen Z sometimes strikes new managers as a "torch the earth" generation who comes in kicking and fighting. But, before you adopt this assumption, it will behoove you to think back to your first job out of high school and college. Remember how exciting and challenging that very first career opportunity was for you? Be careful not to project, but I think in this instance having a bit of empathy for the experience is useful.

---

46 JK Rowling, *Harry Potter and the Half-Blood Prince* (New York, NY: Arthur A. Levine Books, 2005): 470.

One thing you'll want to keep in mind with Generation Z is that they generally don't have a lot of workplace experience, and if you work in a corporate environment, you'll need to carve out some training and management energy for coaching your team members on general workplace etiquette. For example, there's a basic framework for the workplace that they may need help adjusting to, such as the basics of how to participate in a meeting, how to respond to emails, how to dress for an on-site client presentation, how to talk to superiors, and what topics to avoid in the work setting.

If you typically hire people out of college, you may have to do less of this depending on how much internship or job experience they had prior to joining your company. However, it's always best to offer this help from the get-go, especially since you want to be sure to level the playing field as much as possible for young professionals who may not have had the privilege of having these pre-career opportunities. So, pair your Gen Z folks with more seasoned and trusted mentors on your team or across your company, and you'll be planting the seeds for a great career for your team member.

Generation Z, in my experience, places a high value on diversity and alternative leadership models.

This reflects both the demographic diversity in Gen Z[47] as the world becomes more of a melting pot and the relative "wokeness" of this generation. Gen Z employees genuinely want to work, and work hard, for employers they feel are making the world a better place and providing leadership opportunities outside of traditional management careers. I recommend asking your Gen Z team members to take leadership roles right away in making the workplace better and more inclusive. You can also give them

---

47   Kim Parker and Ruth Igielnik, "On the Cusp of Adulthood and Facing an Uncertain Future: What We Know About Gen Z So Far," Pew Research Center, May 14, 2020, https://www.pewresearch.org/social-trends/2020/05/14/on-the-cusp-of-adulthood-and-facing-an-uncertain-future-what-we-know-about-gen-z-so-far-2/.

small, structured, but meaningful, areas of the job to own so they can explore career paths in addition to improving as generalists, which is also important at this stage.

It's likely Gen Z won't have a super clear idea of the type of career they want to pursue yet, and for that reason it's important to actively expose them to different specialties, ideas, and skill sets so they feel invested while they improve across the board. As with other demographics, focus on constructive feedback so you can correct bad habits or misunderstandings as early as possible, but do so especially with Gen Z. They will really appreciate and likely respond well to this mentorship.

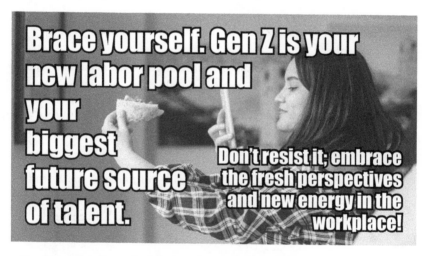

Gen Z is officially in the labor pool and likely the biggest candidate pipeline in your industry in one way or another. Learn how this generation adapts to the workplace and coach them to excellence early.

Finally, with Gen Z, I have noticed a bit of a steadfastness in the workplace that sometimes becomes a "hill to die on" with some situations. Frankly, I think this just comes with having limited life and career experience and not always knowing when it's appropriate to let something go versus sticking to ideals. These traits are not necessarily bad—Gen Z has high ideals and high expectations for their employers, and they will put in the work when it's needed.

But you may need to coach your Gen Z employees to learn how to become a bit more strategic and pragmatic when navigating workplace politics. This is a good opportunity to help guide them towards being effective with their initiatives without burning themselves out too soon or alienating strategic allies in the workplace. This will all come with time. Many of us have learned this the hard way, but give your Gen Z employees a leg up with some focused coaching to keep them challenged, driven, and high performing.

To succeed with your Gen Z employees, keep in mind the following:

- Your Gen Z employees are probably bright, motivated, and talented. Embrace this energy on your team!

- You may need to provide some workplace basics with your Gen Z employees, such as email best practices, how to construct a business email, and how to run a meeting. It's worth the effort!

- Empower your Gen Z employees with cultural and social leadership responsibilities. Asking them to plan a team activity or come up with an icebreaker question for new hires can help channel their energy into outcomes.

- Unlike boomers, Gen Zers are more comfortable communicating behind a screen. Meet them where they're at and don't be afraid to chitchat via instant message to establish a warmth (but remind them of the need to have phone and in-person skills for the real stuff).

To sum up this chapter, your relationships with your team members are like currency, as in any other relationship between two humans. These relationships have a special nature in that it they are rooted in the workplace where more and more people get their primary social, emotional, and intellectual needs met. They also contain a unique set of boundaries and require special privacy and attention that only exist in this special type of relationship—and of course that is between a supervisor and supervisee.

As far as the relationship currency goes, there will be times when you earn it by making meaningful deposits into the trust bank you share. These will be moments where you support your team member behind the scenes, cover them in case of emergency, invest in their sense of security and well-being, and deliver meaningful feedback that can supercharge their career potential.

On the converse, there will be times where you have to spend it—assigning them a yucky project, asking them to reprioritize tasks without having enough time to explain why, or telling them no when they request a raise, PTO that you can't afford to have them take, etc.

Having a positive balance in the trust bank ensures a functional and meaningful relationship for you both, so be sure you are actively leading the way in building up the balance over time.

To do that, you should be mindful of generational differences and the cultural context in which your team members operate. While there is no excuse for stereotyping employees based on their age or other characteristics, understanding a variety of life experiences by generation can be powerful as you navigate communication styles, setting workplace norms and admitting your own weaknesses in being able to relate to a completely different life experience than your own.

chapter 7

BUILDING YOUR #HIVEMIND

"The strength of the team is each individual member. The strength of each member is the team."
—*Phil Jackson*

In 2018, basketball legend Kevin Durant took a nearly $10 million pay cut to play for the Golden State Warriors.[48]

Why?

The modern Golden State Warriors NBA team rivals the Chicago Bulls circa 1996–1997 for the GOAT title in sports history, period. Warriors players know that being part of a winning, legendary team and brand will

---

48   Courtney Connley, "Kevin Durrant took a nearly $10 million pay cut to play for the Warriors— here's why," CNBC, June 7, 2018, https://www.cnbc.com/2018/06/07/why-kevin-durant-took-a-10-million-pay-cut-to-play-for-the-warriors.html.

pay more dividends for them in the long run than optimizing just for compensation.

These great players know what your employees also know: Given that their basic financial needs are being met, the association with a high-performing team with satisfying teamwork and a terrific leader is worth more than a paycheck itself.

Now you are in the position to create, nurture, and support a legendary team. One that is composed of unique and diverse individuals who play off each other's strengths, have each other's backs, and just plain enjoy working together.

Have you heard the saying, "The whole is greater than the sum of its parts"? This is one of those cliches that is 100 percent accurate when it comes to managing a team in the workplace. It's also not at all unique to the current market or time in history.

As a manager, you'll be in a position to steer your team's dynamic towards a common goal, create a dynamic and meaningful professional experience for your individual direct reports and yourself alike, and set yourself up as a respected leader who gets things done.

We see the draw of a high-performing team across industries and contexts, from sports to the military to the government, and you get to make it happen! But how?

Let's start with the fundamentals, the people themselves, as they are the building blocks of a great team.

HIRING THE RIGHT PEOPLE, NOT A RESUME

"Everybody on my team—I couldn't do their jobs. I could not. I really mean that. So, I figured out early on that the way you're successful is you hire really successful people."
—*Carol Bartz*[49]

In chapter 3, we covered some of the operational basics of hiring. You'll need to quickly learn these tactical steps of moving candidates through the pipeline, as this will likely be one of your first official management duties.

But the art of building a team is just as important, if not more so. As illustrated in the Kevin Durant-Golden State Warriors example, the investment you make in the team dynamics and reputation will be one of the most important ways to produce results and create the satisfying, high-performing experience that your team members crave.

And it all starts with hiring.

Hiring is the most important contribution you will make for developing a kick-ass team worthy of envy and in eventually sealing your legacy as a legendary manager.

Why?

Besides the more obvious impacts and operational challenges of undoing a bad hiring decision, the broader implications include introducing negative or toxic energy into your team vibe, creating unhealthy competitiveness, or at worst, bringing people into your team who are abusive towards their peers. Nope.

---

49 Adam Bryant, "Imagining a World of No Annual Reviews," the New York Times, October 17, 2009, https://www.nytimes.com/2009/10/18/business/18corner.html.

To avoid the mistake of a bad hiring decision, you will need to engage your emotional intelligence in addition to your analytical skill set, because each person you bring to the table shifts the game a little bit.

Often, average hiring managers and even recruiters are looking to replicate a prior hiring success by seeking out and hiring people who match a certain profile, whether that be an educational alignment, specific job experience, or other factors. Of course, when you're in an industry where you need a specific and explicit qualification, such as medicine, construction, or some other licensed profession, you shouldn't skimp out or compromise on these fundamentals.

That said, keep in mind that many of the jobs in today's knowledge and creative economy don't always require specific technical skills, as they're becoming more and more fluid. Based on your industry, the requirements themselves often evolve.

For these reasons, I encourage you to think of your hiring decisions as an optimization exercise that results in bringing someone into your team who represents a demographic, perspective, or skill set that you don't already have. Although this may seem counterintuitive if you've had one successful hiring profile, you do often get diminishing marginal returns for each consecutive hire who meets that profile.

For example, if you are building a product-marketing team, without question you'll want your first hire to be someone who has solid industry experience. You'll want someone you know has a track record of executing on marketing projects and who can take the reins. Obviously, you'll get a huge ROI (return on investment) with those attributes as your first hire.

For your second hire, you may want to go in another direction. Perhaps your first hire is great at strategy but struggles with day-to-day executions. So, for your next hire, you may want to look for someone with less marketing experience who wants to break into marketing and is willing to quarterback the daily grind while they learn the trade.

Or maybe the marketing gurus on your team lack industry experience for the industry your company is selling into, so you may want to think about bringing someone in right from that industry to share their insider knowledge with your team and who can learn the ropes from the marketing vets.

Perhaps you've hired a lot of marketing people who are millennials but you're selling B2B (business-to-business) software to older executives, so it might be time to start thinking about hiring a Gen Xer or boomer to provide some guiding expertise on connecting with the older executive audience.

Maybe your marketing team is, frankly, all white people, and you might prioritize hiring a person of color to offer another perspective and provide that all-important sanity check that your messaging is hitting the mark and isn't tone deaf.

To stick with the marketing example, it's true that in recent history there's been more than one embarrassing marketing gaffe from companies that put out a product or ad that caused a controversy. Remember the Gucci sweater that resembled blackface? [50] Yikes!

Would this have happened if there had been Black marketing professionals on the staff?

To extend the example into other industries, we know that products reflect the implicit bias of the people who create those products. Several high-profile incidents have happened in the self-driving car industry or facial recognition software, for example, in which these cars have crashed into Black

---

50 Amy Held, "Gucci Apologizes And Removes Sweater Following 'Blackface' Backlash," NPR, February 7, 2019, https://www.npr.org/2019/02/07/692314950/gucci-apologizes-and-removes-sweater-following-blackface-backlash.

people at a higher rate than white people. [51] Could these have been avoided had the hiring managers at these car companies been focused on hiring people who expanded the team's hivemind, rather than a carbon copy of a profile that's worked in the past?

Throw out the phrase "culture fit" and replace it with "culture add." Homogeneity is the bedfellow of blandness at best and unintentionally racist or sexist products at worst.

The bottom line: Hire people, not resumes.

REFERENCE CHECKS: WHY YOU SHOULD DO THEM

I'm guessing that at some point in your adult life, you've been asked to provide references of some kind. Maybe this is for housing, an internship, a college recommendation letter, etc. And when you were thinking through

---

51   Mark Matousek, "A new study found that self-driving vehicles may have a harder time detecting people with dark skin, and it could point to a bigger issue with how the technology is tested," Business Insider, March 6, 2019, https://www.businessinsider.com/self-driving-cars-worse-at-detecting-dark-skin-study-says-2019-3.

which people in your life to ask for this favor, you didn't pick people you suspected would speak ill of you.

So, given the fact that nobody in their right mind is going to submit a reference that does not think highly of the individual in question, you may think, What's the point? You would be right in regard to your substandard, low-effort reference check, but let me explain why you should still do them and take them seriously.

Reference checks are like the last line of defense, and by the time someone is at this stage, you've likely spoken to them many times and are nearly ready to proceed. So, why go through this process?

Through an effective reference screening, you can extrapolate the following:

- Learn anything that can disqualify the candidate.
- Trust but verify the interview answers were accurate (hello, Ronald Reagan!).
- Learn how candidates do their best work and their worst work.
- Understand how you can support them as a manager to be most effective.
- Understand how the candidate deals with conflicts.
- Get an objective take on the unique skills or background the candidate brings to the team.

Once your candidates are in the final stages of hiring and you've asked them to supply two to three references, I suggest using the following general outline for handling these reference-screening calls.

Introduction (three to five minutes) to build rapport. Ask the reference how they know the individual in question, for how long, and in what capacity.

Performance questions:

Why was Tarik hired into this role? Did that come true?

What are some words you would use to describe Tarik?

Can you give me an example where Tarik took initiative?

What were Tarik's strong points, and where were his weak points?

Team-vibe questions:

When things aren't going to plan, how does Tarik communicate that with his peers?

How does Tarik deal with an ambitious goal and pressure?

What unique qualities does Tarik offer a team?

How would Tarik's peers describe what it was like to work with him?

Is Tarik more process driven or relationship driven?

How does Tarik take personal feedback? Any stories?

How does Tarik handle when an executive decision is made that he doesn't agree with?

Manager-style questions:

What is Tarik's temperament in difficult situations?

How technical is Tarik? Does Tarik thrive in solving complex problems?

How does Tarik do with details and schedules?

How much autonomy should I give Tarik?

What advice would you give to a future manager of Tarik?

It is quite unlikely that by the time someone gets to this stage the references alone are what sours you on a candidate, but it has happened! Any time the answers to these questions seemed weak or if someone had any hesitation and I made an offer, it turned out 10 times worse. As you'll learn, a bad hiring decision is one of the worst things you can do in your quest to develop a team of all-stars.

The bottom line: To create a team that rivals the Golden State Warriors, hire great people, not just great resumes, and be thoughtful about the composition of your team by recruiting and hiring people who add different perspectives and skill sets. Reference checks are an irreplaceable part of that process and are worth the effort to decrease the risk of making a bad hiring decision.

DIVERSITY AND INCLUSION

"No matter what he does, every person on earth plays a central role in the history of the world."
—Paulo Coelho, *The Alchemist*[52]

It's hard to learn modern management theory without hearing the phrase diversity and inclusion (D&I) these days. Frankly, it's become such a buzzword (buzzphrase? Is that a thing?) that it's almost lost its meaning.

But you and I know that it's critical to get right with your moral compass when it comes to equality in the workplace, and it turns out that embracing the principles of D&I will also make you a rock-star leader and enable your team to perform better than ever.

Wait, what?

Yep. D&I efforts and outcomes are critical to staying ahead of the game for any company, as multiple studies repeatedly show us that diverse teams

---

52   Paul Coelho, *The Alchemist* (New York, NY: HarperOne, 2015): 158

perform better and produce optimal results.[53] At this point, that really shouldn't be a controversial statement, as this is a widely held conclusion in business.

Beyond the short-term outcomes of diverse teams, investing in D&I on your team will help attract millennials and Gen Zers to your team and will position you as a strong leader in your organization.[54]

It's a win-win, so why aren't more teams more diverse?

The fact is, it takes some intention and extra work up front to create diverse teams. It's simply not the path of least resistance in many cases. But you can make it happen.

Firstly, it's important to understand that diversity and inclusion are two separate words because they're two separate concepts, albeit tightly intertwined.

Diversity is easy to measure, as it is simply the demographic breakdown of staff that represents certain characteristics, whatever you are trying to measure.

Inclusion, in contrast, can be described as the sense of belonging that your staff feels and experiences in the workplace. Although both can be captured by metrics, diversity is easier to describe numerically, whereas inclusion is much harder as it's significantly more qualitative.

When we think of measuring diversity in the workplace, we typically start with an analysis of representation amongst a population as compared to the distribution of that group in the broader population. We usually begin

---

53   David Rock and Heidi Grant, "Why Diverse Teams Are Smarter," Harvard Business Review, November 4, 2016, https://hbr.org/2016/11/why-diverse-teams-are-smarter.
54   "Here's Why Millennials Want More Diverse Workplaces," Kudos, December 10, 2019, https://www.kudos.com/resource/blog/heres-why-millennials-want-more-diverse-workplaces/.

the analysis by looking at the numbers reflected by two broadly underrepresented groups: women and non-white people.

Since women are roughly 50 percent of the American population, and non-white people are 40 percent[55] (ish, depending on how you measure this, which is part of the challenge), we should see roughly that level of representation in each industry, at all levels of management, right? Hah! Well, it doesn't take a rocket scientist to see that this is nowhere near the case in most industries, although many have made impressive strides in the past decade. You might be thinking, well, why doesn't the level of representation reflect the population?

The answer to that is beyond the scope of this book, although I strongly encourage further reading on these subjects. It will only broaden your worldview and understanding of your place in this social-justice puzzle as a new hiring manager with the newfound power you wield.

As a first-time manager, your role in creating a diverse workplace is paramount. Hiring managers are the most important variable, in my experience, for cultivating the kind of diversity that can move the needle here. No amount of HR intervention, leadership directions, government programs, etc. can make the kind of immediate and lasting change that occurs simply when you hire and manage in a way that creates diverse teams and equal opportunities to advance.

This won't be easy—many hiring managers complain about the pipeline problem and other factors that make it difficult to find qualified candidates who: 1) know about your open requisitions, and 2) are interested and willing to apply.

---

55   William H. Frey, "The Nation Is Diversifying Even Faster Than Predicted, According to New Census Data," The Brookings Institution, July 1, 2020, https://www.brookings.edu/research/new-census-data-shows-the-nation-is-diversifying-even-faster-than-predicted/.

If you're not familiar with the term, the Pipeline Problem essentially summarizes the view that not enough minorities or underrepresented communities exist at any point in the pipeline of talent—the underrepresentation starting with unequal access to quality education and STEM-related topics at a young age and the divergence in achievements that originates in early life, leading to further disparities as employable adults.

By the time adults are ready for the job market, the cycle of poverty, uneven access, and lack of opportunity has been years in the making and is so deeply entrenched in society that it is impossible to turn the tide at the point of a hiring decision. In other words, because the scarcity of underrepresented professionals has been years in the making (of course, no fault of the hiring manager! It's a system-wide issue, right?), it is simply impossible to correct for these inequities because qualified candidates are nowhere to be found.

To help unpack and overcome some of these challenges, let's start with the first assumption that there are no qualified candidates. Of course there are qualified candidates.

If you find yourself thinking these thoughts (and we all do), put those to the wind because that just isn't true. Once we can agree that this statement isn't true, we can start to do more meaningful work on the diversity "problem" by working on the two complicating factors mentioned previously and by acknowledging that they are, in fact, real challenges: 1) qualified candidates not knowing about job opportunities at your company, and 2) finding candidates who are interested and willing to apply.

So, how then do we bridge the gap between diverse, qualified candidates and your hiring pipeline? Let's start with how you are posting and informing the general public about your open roles. Depending on what industry you work in, it may be that the information about your open head count is only available to industry insiders. This commonly happens in tech where it's not unusual to promote from within or create strong financial incentives for employee referrals, which are both tempting options to fill positions quickly, especially during times of hypergrowth.

Unfortunately, both programs often lead to a lack of diversity, since people generally associate themselves with people like themselves, and so hiring an outsider rather than promoting internally or giving additional weight to an employee referral can often exacerbate the diversity problem. So, as you take the reigns as a hiring manager, make sure you understand the implications of these programs.

You should also think about where you're posting open job roles. It's one thing to list a job on your company website, but to really open up your talent pool, I recommend partnering with professional networking groups that actively facilitate connections with underrepresented groups. If your company doesn't work with any, find some yourself on Google or LinkedIn. Most professions have some sort of minority networking group in that industry and nothing's stopping you from simply reaching out and asking if someone can post your open rec. Also, actively ask your family and friends who are in minority groups to post the job rec on their social networks.

Get creative! The heavy lifting you do up front makes it a lot easier to get diverse talent into your pipeline, which will pay dividends in the long run.

In chapter 9, we will take a deeper dive specifically into how to use your position as a manager to work towards racial equality. For now, here are some of the key points as you think about creating a badass, diverse team that represents the United States today—it's your job to do your part to make this happen!

- Learn and internalize the business case for diversity and be ready to repeat it often.

- Have open discussions about inclusion with your team and ensure you're getting feedback on their sense of belonging.

- Ensure there is broad and equitable distribution of your job descriptions.

- Nurture a diverse professional network yourself so when you are ready to hire, you have an ecosystem of diverse talent that is familiar with your company and team.

CULTURE, CULTURE, CULTURE

"Culture eats strategy for breakfast."
—Unknown

I know this chapter has been rife with metaphors and hyperbole, but bear with me while I surface another one that is relevant here: Culture eats strategy for breakfast (not to be confused with Wheaties is the Breakfast of Champions—that's a whole other thing).

At some point in your career, you've likely worked in an organization or department that you would describe as toxic, so you know that these environments make you want to run for the hills and plan an exit strategy in every break you have. I'm sure you wouldn't say you've done the best work of your career in this environment or felt particularly motivated to go above and beyond for that employer or manager.

As the head of your department or team, you will be an essential ingredient in cultivating a functional, inclusive, and unique culture for the group you lead, as well as influence the greater company culture for the better. Culture, ultimately, will make or break your team's performance and will be the social glue that makes the job worth it for your team.

In fact, culture is what makes the difference between a department and a team.

Culture is what will transform your employees from a worker mentality to an owner mentality (if your company pays in stock options, frankly, they are owners). It is what your employees will say about your org and each other to their friends and family and how they represent your employer brand to the community.

Culture doesn't just stop at the social aspects of the team—it is also reflected in the professional aspects of your workplace. It is the collection of unspoken rules that influences your work habits and conduct. Some examples of these may include norms for participating in meetings, work hours, workplace dress code, the culture around lunch breaks, and whether emails on weekends is appropriate.

I'm not going to tell you how to define these cultural norms for your own team—your job is to analyze and weigh what you specifically want to normalize against what the trends are in your industry—but I am advising you to be intentional and observant about what you're creating.

As the leader, you'll be the primary influence as to what these cultural norms are, and your team needs to know that this is a priority for you. Otherwise, they won't take culture seriously themselves, and this can lead to burnout, toxicity, and overall meh feelings about the work and the team (nothing Kevin Durant would take a $10 million pay cut to be a part of).

How do you show your team that you make culture a priority?

After you've established some baseline trust and camaraderie with your employees—within the first month or so of your tenure—you should have honest and candid conversations about your team, company, and industry culture as you grow into your new role, take the reins, and listen to what your team is saying.

Ask them what they value most in the workplace and unpack any negative experiences they've had in this job or in previous roles. Really actively listen. Don't just listen to respond, but listen to learn. Repeat back what you think you are hearing and reflect on it for a couple of days before taking any action you think is needed.

Live the culture yourself!

You will be under a microscope during your first 90 days or so in your new role, and the way you conduct yourself during this time will set a tone for the unwritten rules of the team that will long outlive your tenure as the leader.

So, if you don't think it's good to write emails on weekends, don't write emails on weekends. (Pro tip: You can still write them and use Outlook or Gmail plug-in to schedule the emails for a reasonable hour.)

Do you want to infuse fun into your culture? Be freakin' fun! Hold a dad-joke competition in your Slack channel, do a photo competition, Rick roll your team meetings.

Do you want to tighten up your culture to adhere to better timelines for projects? Adhere to timelines for projects yourself. When you commit to getting something done for your team or for your own work, get it done on time and make sure it's visible how you're doing it.

In order to further invest in team building, plan activities regularly. Your team needs time to come together outside of the day-to-day work to create shared memories. The best team-building activities take people just outside of their comfort zone as a group and as individuals. Something like improv, a talent show, or taking a cooking class together are great ideas for doing so. These should also be inclusive and culturally and lifestyle appropriate for everyone on the team. Be mindful of serving alcohol if you've got someone with a known addiction issue, having too many after-hours events if you have working parents, or scheduling something highly physical if you have employees with disabilities.

For remote teams, an investment into team-building activities is important, too. Following are a few ideas for culture-building remote-team activities:

- Photo scavenger hunt challenge (post a photo *of* a photo that you can find in your kitchen).

- Trivia or other games that can be played virtually.

- Physically mailing ingredients for a recipe you'll all try to make.

- Remote dance tutorial or yoga class.

But don't overthink it. Ask your team for suggestions! These events are when you'll find your team creating inside jokes, expressing their individuality, exploring creativity, learning how to communicate, and developing the bonds they'll need to get through the hard times together. Work with your leadership and HR partners to develop a budget for activities like this. A regular, intentional investment in culture will pay off in dividends.

As a rule of thumb, I recommend some sort of casual, shorter team builder every three to four months, with something more substantial once or twice a year. I also encourage spontaneous and mini culture-building activities sprinkled throughout your normal work cadence. For example, start a team meeting with an ice-breaker question (What was the name of your first pet? What song do you remember most from middle school?) and seasonal-specific events like a costume contest for Halloween, an office Olympics during the actual Olympics, or a team screening of a favorite movie.

In designing team-building activities, the key is to select activities that are engaging, fun, and just challenging enough to push your team members right up to the edge of their comfort zone. Through subtle discomfort in a super safe environment (think improv or taking a watercolor class), social bonds are apt to form, which are the right ingredients for a fun culture. Shared new experiences lead to all the good bits of fun that are the foundation for just enough of a social trust on your team.

And that trust leads to professional trust and the feeling of accountability. [56] The feeling of having each other's backs is what we as humans crave so deeply from our work, no matter what field we're in. So, get creative and invest in team building!

You can't just rely on perks and the cool factor of your company to retain and motivate your employees; you have to create authentic culture to foster a positive working environment.

---

56   Neelam Saraswat and Shilpi Khandelwal, "Impact of Team Building Exercises on Team Effectiveness," International Journal of marketing and Human Resource Management (IJMHRM) 6, no.3 (Sep - Dec, 2015), 89–97, http://www.iaeme.com/MasterAdmin/UploadFolder/IJMHRM_06_03_010/IJMHRM_06_03_010.pdf.

To create the absolute best culture possible, do the following:

- Determine what behaviors you'd like to normalize as the unwritten rules of your team.

- Live these yourself *first*, and then socialize with your team.

- Take care to communicate thoughtfully and utilize active listening to create a sense of psychological safety—a fundamental aspect of good work culture.

- Regularly invest in team-building activities that create just enough laughter and challenge to add juice to the social lubricant that greases the wheels of teamwork.

chapter 8

IT'S ALL ABOUT YOU (NO, REALLY)

"Be yourself, everybody else is already taken."
—Unknown

Stop reading this book right now and put your name into Google. What comes up? Which photos appear? What will your team, your company, and your boss think about you based on these results?

If you have some less-than-flattering results show up (hello, Jello-shot party from college that the internet will show forever), don't worry even one iota. This means you've lived a life. And it also means that lots of internet people will know that about you.

You might be thinking, I am so much more than my Google search results and abandoned Myspace page! Just have one conversation with me. I'll show you who I am!

And you would be right, of course. You are so much more than your Google search results.

If you sat down to have a conversation with someone, what would you say? What would you wear? Would you meet at a coffee shop, a bar, a park? What part of your life story would you condense into a casual conversation to create a different sense of reality about who you are outside of what the internet says?

As you take this next step in your career, more than ever, you should take stock of your personal brand and set some clear goals for yourself in developing this further.

But why does it even matter to your job? It's called a personal brand, not a professional brand, right?

It actually matters a lot. Your personal brand will set the tone for how your team responds to your leadership and will pave the way for getting what you need to make the team, and ultimately yourself, succeed. And, as a new leader of a team of people, your example and leadership style matter just as much as who you are.

Can you effectively say who you are? If you can't, your team, your peers, and leadership will answer it for you, for better or for worse! So, let's break it down and explore your personal brand and how it intersects and guides you and your team in this new management structure.

A personal brand is, essentially, your reputation. It's composed of what others say about you, just as you do about other leaders. As humans, it's in our nature to judge, and that's not necessarily a bad thing. Although being judgement-free in a sense is a respectable ideal, the type of judgement I am talking about here is more about leveraging, and in some cases, hacking people's built-in perception system to build your rapport and effectiveness, and create a meaningful picture of who you are that enables you to lead like the lovely human you are.

A brand is so much more than a logo. It's a feeling. It's a presence. It's impact. Think of the feeling you get when you see familiar brands, and how these companies have affected you and your community's life. I want you to think about an image of a black check mark on a white surface. A bright red bull's-eye. A solid blue circle with a lowercase f inscribed. What companies do you associate these images with? What impact have these companies had on your life and your community? You can see how these brands are so much more than logos.

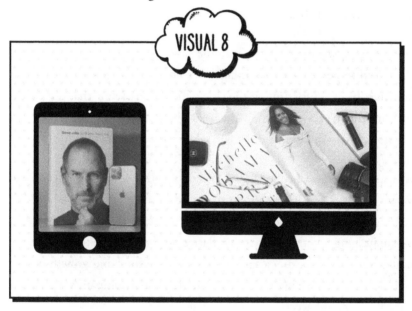

Can a person be a brand? Absolutely, the same things apply! It's a feeling; it's a presence; it's impact. Think of the feeling you get when you see these people and how they have affected you and your community's life.

What are your thoughts on Steve Jobs, and Michelle Obama?

Gosh! You're so judgey!

It's not a bad thing, though. Any sensations or sentiments in your head around companies or individuals are essentially judgements you are assigning to those companies or people. The word judgement has an implication of negativity. We call people judgmental to indicate that a person must have some holier-than-thou attitude towards others, and prefer to think of ourselves as being nonjudgmental people in the sense that we accept everyone, right?

Sorry to say it, but you are just as judgey as the next Karen, and once you accept that reality you can unpack your cognitive tendencies to judge to better define your personal brand, knowing that literally everyone is judging you, just a little bit, and not necessarily in a negative way.

To break it down further, let's examine how humans create judgements, which lead to perceptions. An infant does not have judgement yet, and so they must be cared for around the clock. They don't know that hot things will burn them; they don't know that that uncomfortable feeling is hunger; they don't know that they need a nap when they are cranky.

As an adult, we have a collection of experiences that form our judgements. We are constantly judging the world around us merely to survive in it. We are judging the speed of oncoming traffic to decide if it's safe to proceed. We are judging whether our clothes flatter our body shape to decide if we should buy them. We are judging a company's culture and growth potential based on what we know about the market and a company's reputation to see if we should accept a job offer there.

Like it or not, people are talking about you, and now that you're a manager you'll be even more scrutinized and gossiped about. Get used to it! The sooner you accept that this is your new normal, the better off you'll be in learning how to manage this.

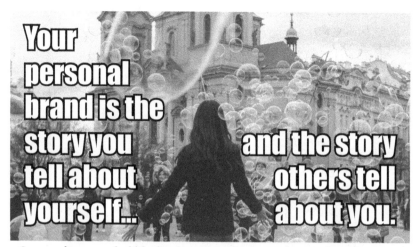

Your personal brand is the story you tell about yourself... and the story others tell about you.

Sorry to bust your bubble, but your reputation is pretty much your personal brand. And you have one, whether you like it or not!

It can certainly be hard stepping into the limelight a little more than you may have been used to in the past. That said, it has already been happening, I promise you, and if you don't believe me, ask yourself how you were identified as someone who was ready to become a manager. It's because people are talking about you. People are talking about your reputation. You have a brand already!

Take stock of your personal brand as you move into a formal leadership role by doing an audit of your online presence, your professional and personal network, your style and taste, and your physical presence. Don't be afraid! Google yourself and check which parts of your social media are visible to the public; check which online forums you've participated in; ask people close to you what you're known for and how you present yourself.

To develop a personal brand, focus on the above categories and in turn, you will become a more interesting and intriguing leader.

Don't obsess, but do approach these questions with a curious mind, so you can be self-aware of what it's like to experience you. Whatever you discover, these are the building blocks to your brand that will play into how you are perceived as a leader. Set a few goals for how you'd like to further develop your brand and encourage your team to do the same. Do you want to speak at a conference? Deliver a particular work project ahead of schedule? Start a personal blog? Get involved with a nonprofit? Find a really great work sneaker? Whatever it is, write it down and start making it happen. It all matters and it all adds up. This is a never-ending process, as you'll continuously discover new things about yourself as you work towards your goals.

What do you want to be remembered for? What would they remember you for now?

The difference between those "whats" is your goal.

IMPOSTER SYNDROME

"You are perfectly cast in your life. I can't imagine
anyone but you in the role. Go play."
—Lin-Manuel Miranda [57]

Ahh, imposter syndrome, my old friend, and quite likely yours, too! Let's be real, is there anybody who takes on a manager role and doesn't experience imposter syndrome?

In a nutshell, imposter syndrome describes the nagging feeling or negative thought pattern that accompanies professional accomplishments, such as a promotion, and is particularly prevalent in women and minorities. This is

---

57 Tweet by @Lin_Manuel, April 29, 2016, https://twitter.com/lin_manuel/status/726025564696502272?lang=en.

likely due to some combination of internalized sexism, racism, homophobia, you name it. [58]

While imposter syndrome doesn't quite go away, it is an important thing to effectively manage in your new role so you can thrive. Part of that is making peace with its presence and influence on your thoughts.

An instinct to combat imposter syndrome can involve spending hours reading, practicing, working hard on gaining skills, or achieving milestones in life to prove to yourself that you are deserving of your status in life. While far be it for me to discourage anybody from setting ambitious professional or personal goals, I don't believe this alone will suffice to quell the negative feelings that imposter syndrome tends to provoke.

My advice for combating imposter syndrome is twofold: The first is more tactical and the second is more holistic.

Imposter syndrome, while not in and of itself a diagnosable condition, is a bedfellow of more acute disorders such as anxiety or depression, where the sufferer internalizes and eventually believes negative self-talk or illogical postures about the world to the point where they are paralyzed in their efforts to live a fulfilling, pleasant life. [59] As such, similar principles can be applied to reduce the noise from the ongoing chatter of negativity.

To break this down, someone who suffers from an anxiety or depressive disorder may experience a slew of intrusive, negative thoughts: Something terrible is going to happen if I don't get an A in this class. I'm never going to find a spouse. To the disordered mind, these thoughts are indistinguish-

58   Sheryl Nance-Nash, "Why Imposter Syndrome Hits Women and Women of Colour Harder," BBC, July 27, 2020, https://www.bbc.com/worklife/article/20200724-why-imposter-syndrome-hits-women-and-women-of-colour-harder.

59   Kirsten Weir, "Feel Like a Fraud?" American Psychology Association, accessed May 18, 2021, https://www.apa.org/gradpsych/2013/11/fraud.

able from reality and create an emotional environment where they overwhelm the sufferer.

The principles of cognitive behavioral therapy (CBT) are a known effective method for addressing and managing these intrusive, happiness-limiting thoughts and can be applied to the negative self-talk occurring in the mind of someone experiencing imposter syndrome. [60] CBT implores us to leverage our innate logician and scrupulous inner wisdom to examine these passing thoughts with an objective sniff test and to work actively to accept the results of this examination as the more trustworthy probable truth.

For example, apply this analysis to an anxious thought of worrying about your spouse dying in a motorcycle accident the next time they go on a ride. You can accept that there is some inherent risk involved with riding a motorcycle, but that the probability remains low and therefore isn't worth occupying the space it's given in your mind. Thus, through applied CBT, one can actively work to accept the more likely reality that they probably won't die in a motorcycle accident as the hierarchical dominating thought rather than the anxious-mind inner chatter that tends to assume the worst.

If you apply a similar analysis to thoughts about your performance in your professional role, you will probably arrive at a conclusion that is closer to reality. This may be something like, I am generally successful at my job and have qualifying credentials to rise to the challenge, even though sometimes I'm not great at X. To reinforce this narrative, it can be helpful to ask for objective feedback from trusted peers who you know won't blow smoke up your ass. Given that you trust their professional opinion, you can train your brain to absorb their fair feedback as a decent analysis of your skills and talents.

---

60 Michael Grothaus, "How to Master Your Brain to Overcome Imposter Syndrome," Fast Company, February, 27, 2017, https://www.fastcompany.com/3068415/how-to-master-your-brain-to-overcome-impostor-syndrome.

Presumably, part of why you earned the promotion into management is your ability to be self-reflective, embrace humility, and take critical feedback on the chin. It turns out that many of these same qualities are the other side of the imposter syndrome coin. The challenge is to keep the needle towards the humility side of the spectrum, but not push it over the edge to where deeply held insecurities cause an overcompensation of confidence that reduces your effectiveness.

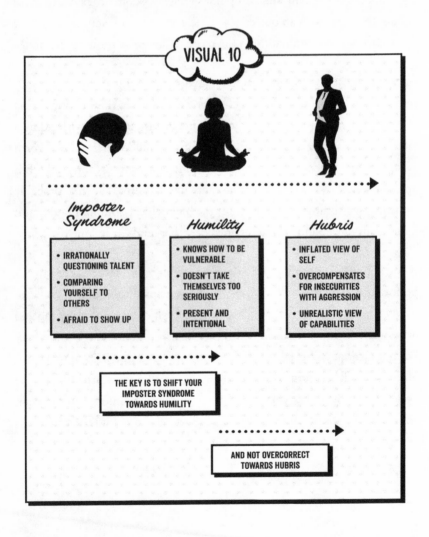

VISUAL 10

Imposter Syndrome

- IRRATIONALLY QUESTIONING TALENT
- COMPARING YOURSELF TO OTHERS
- AFRAID TO SHOW UP

Humility

- KNOWS HOW TO BE VULNERABLE
- DOESN'T TAKE THEMSELVES TOO SERIOUSLY
- PRESENT AND INTENTIONAL

Hubris

- INFLATED VIEW OF SELF
- OVERCOMPENSATES FOR INSECURITIES WITH AGGRESSION
- UNREALISTIC VIEW OF CAPABILITIES

THE KEY IS TO SHIFT YOUR IMPOSTER SYNDROME TOWARDS HUMILITY

AND NOT OVERCORRECT TOWARDS HUBRIS

For me personally, my imposter syndrome is the fiercest right before public speaking, especially in front of a group of people I really admire or aspire to be. Let's say I'm speaking at a conference for women in business. Thoughts like these race through my head: Why did they pick you to give this talk? Couldn't they have found a better or more qualified presenter?

As these intrusive thoughts start spiraling, I will counter them with other, more logical ones: They asked me to give this talk because they want to know what I think, and Yes, there are more accomplished people than I am out there, but I've accomplished a lot, too, and have important things to say that this group will benefit from hearing.

After the talk, I will ask a trusted member of the audience to tell me honestly and with conviction what went well and what could have made it even better. I accept that feedback earnestly and try to kick more ass the next time. And so forth and so on.

Embrace your imposter syndrome for what it is—a balancing force that prevents us from dipping too far into hubris as leaders. The goal is to keep this inner critic in check but not completely drowned out by overcompensating thoughts.

YOU AND YOUR TEAM'S BRAND

"Talent wins games, but teamwork and intelligence win championships."
—Michael Jordan [61]

What person's name is the first that comes to your mind when you think about Tesla?

---

61   Michael Jordan, I Can't Accept Not Trying: Michael Jordan on the Pursuit of Excellence (San Francisco, CA: HarperSanFrancisco, 1994): 20.

What about *O* magazine?

The slogan "Make America Great Again"?

If you thought, Elon Musk, Oprah Winfrey, and Donald Trump consecutively, you wouldn't be alone. Your brain made those mental associations without even consciously thinking about it.

The broader point of this mini mental exercise that quite possibly gave you anxiety is that quite often, an organization's overall brand is at least in part defined by the personal brand of its leader. On the extreme end, this might resemble a cult of personality, and this, of course, isn't the goal, but clearly there is a correlation here.

Just as you have your own personal brand, your team will, too, and it will be tied with the type of person you represent yourself to be. You are now at the center of your team's universe, and it's going to be up to you to lead your new team in the direction most beneficial for the company's performance and for your team members' individual careers.

So, your team brand is essentially the collective sum of all the individual parts, over time, with you at the center.

In the previous chapter, we explored your team's culture and how you can develop and invest in it as the leader, and this is certainly a big part of your team's brand. Another component, and the foundation of it all, is their performance, both individually and as a group. There's no way around this—both you and your team need to be producing results in order to progress to the next level. It is going to take good old-fashioned hard work to get there! There just is no shortcut.

So, when you take the reins, ensure you are clear with your own management on what is expected of your team and at what cadence. You should have a good sense of what would be both an attainable measure of performance and a stretch goal, and your team generally should be aligned with these measures.

It is also wise to develop a team mission statement that is deliberate, connected to the overall company's mission statement, and reflective of the values and ambitions of the individual members. As a leader, it will be up to you to facilitate this, and then to market it to the rest of the company through your communication channels. Work with your leader and across other teams to identify opportunities to make this happen.

Is there an upcoming all-hands department meeting where you could present your team charter and goals? Or better yet, do you have a strong leader on your team who you could charge with this responsibility?

In summary, your team will have a brand for better or for worse, and you'll be at the forefront of this. To ensure you're setting the team up for the best success possible with their collective reputation, remember the following:

- Be very clear with your own management on what metrics your team is expected to achieve and in what time period, communicate that openly with your team to align with your mission, and collectively decide on *how* you intend to get there.

- Consider developing a team mission statement that is adjacent to your overall company mission statement, but also unique to your own team's specialty.

- Be yourself and be conscious to avoid having your team culture revolve around a cult of personality.

So, what can a good team brand do for you?

This is the story of a barrier-breaking world champion who left a winning team to join a losing team, and it has three elements: a sport, the teams, and a driver. First, the sport. When you hear Formula 1, do you think chemistry? No? You aren't alone. Most Americans like Formula 1 (F1) about as much as they like mayo on fries: It's fine if you're European, but ketchup for me, please!

However, F1 is the most prestigious category of car racing and one of the most popular sports worldwide. [62] Each race generates about 10 times more revenue than an average NFL game generates [63] and has twice the viewership of the most popular Super Bowl in history. F1 has roots in rich European princes and playboys building sleek, shiny, one-off race cars to best each other around the narrow streets of Monaco.

You'd expect the cars to be fast—and you'd be right. They can reach speeds of around 220 mph [64] and corner so fast that the drivers weigh eight times their body weight in a turn. [65] That's more than twice what astronauts experience during a launch! [66]

Second, the teams. Ferrari is the most successful team in F1 history. Their scarlet, rosso corsa–painted cars have racked up over 238 race wins, 16 constructors' championships, [67] and 15 drivers' championships. [68] The second-most winning team is Team McLaren. They've won 182 races and 20 world championships. Any driver would consider a spot on either team to be the achievement of a lifetime!

---

62 Brad Spurgeon, "Is Formula One Still on Top?" the New York Times, March 18, 2016, https://www.nytimes.com/2016/03/19/sports/autoracing/is-formula-one-still-on-top.html.

63 "F1 generates more revenue per event than any other sport," Motorsport.com, June 12, 2008, https://us.motorsport.com/f1/news/f1-generates-more-revenue-per-event-than-any-sport/2710309/.

64 Anna Duxbury, "How fast is an F1 car? Top speeds of F1, IndyCar, MotoGP and more," Motosport, March 23, 2021, https://www.autosport.com/f1/news/how-fast-is-an-f1-car-top-speeds-of-f1-indycar-motogp-and-more-4980734/4980734/.

65 Brian Silvestro, "The New F1 Cars Pull Nearly 8g in the Corners," Road & Track, March 27, 2017, https://www.roadandtrack.com/motorsports/a33043/the-new-f1-cars-are-nearing-8g-of-lateral-acceleration-in-the-corners/.

66 Ames Research Center, "The Pull of Hypergravity," NASA, accessed May 18, 2021, https://www.nasa.gov/missions/science/hyper.html.

67 "Most World Constructors' Championships," Mostly F1, accessed May 20, 2021, https://www.mostlyf1.com/statistics/all-time-stats/constructor-stats/most-world-constructors-championships/.

68 "Ferrari F1 Team info & statistics," F1 Fansite, accessed May 20, 2021, https://www.f1-fansite.com/f1-teams/ferrari-f1-information-statistics/.

But it's the 21st century, and neither Ferrari nor McLaren has won a championship since 2008. What happened?!

Das Deutsche happened.

In particular, the Mercedes F1 team happened. Until 2010, Mercedes had only competed in F1 in the 1950s. But in 2010, Mercedes decided to return to F1 at long last, and had their sights on beating both Ferrari and McLaren. [69] But alas, the return hadn't really been successful, and they hadn't won much. Ferrari and McLaren were still the teams to beat.

Third, the driver. His name is Lewis Hamilton, and he is the most successful driver in the history of the sport, with seven world titles (at the time of this writing). [70] He pulls in around $50 million a year, making him the 13th highest-paid athlete in the world. [71]

He is also the first—and only—Black driver in F1 history. [72]

His story is remarkable. He came from a working-class town in England and was bullied as a kid for his race. He won the British karting championship at age 10 while his father worked four jobs to support him, and he eventually became the then-youngest driver to win an F1 World Championship in 2008.

Fast-forward to 2013 and Hamilton hadn't won a title for five years, but he was still winning individual races and often in cars slower than his com-

---

69 "F1 2010: Mercedes Grand Prix to return," Racecar Engineering, 2009, https://www.racecar-engineering.com/articles/f1-2010-mercedes-grand-prix-to-return/.

70 Greg Stuart, "From the most wins in F1 history to the most experienced driver – 8 amazing records that were broken in 2002," F1, December 30, 2020, https://www.formula1.com/en/latest/article.from-the-most-wins-in-f1-history-to-the-most-experienced-driver-8-amazing.3A86CsgEsom8jR7ZLgKwkx.html.

71 Kurt Badenhausen, "Highest-Paid Athletes in the World," Forbes, May 21, 2020, https://www.forbes.com/athletes/#6e4ef3d155ae.

72 Luke Smith, "Lewis Hamilton Is Demanding Change," the New York Times, August 7, 2020, https://www.nytimes.com/2020/08/07/sports/autoracing/lewis-hamilton-formula-1-diversity.html.

petition. His career was looking alright, all things considered. The F1 fanbase figured he just needed to stick with it with McLaren, and his chances would improve. After all, McLaren was a winning team, right?

Suddenly, to everyone's shock, Hamilton announced he was leaving McLaren for Mercedes. What?! How could Mercedes possibly give Hamilton a winning car when they hadn't won a championship since 1955? Everyone thought he was nuts, committing career suicide of some kind.

So, why did he do it?

In his own words, "I want to be part of this journey where Mercedes are the most successful Formula one team in history...I think it would really upset the red cars and the red team [Ferrari] so that's my goal..." [73] It turned out to be a smart move, but what was so attractive about this team that it could motivate a world champion to leave a winning team for a team that was losing, race after freakin' race?

A man named Toto Wolff leads Mercedes, and he is a famously unorthodox F1 team manager. In a world of hot-headed drivers and hyper-focused engineers, Wolff has his entire team practice mindfulness. "We have actually rolled out meditation across the whole team—over 1,000 people," Wolff has said. Another key to their culture is what Wolff terms a "see it, say it, fix it" and "no blame" culture. [74]

Looking at the leadership and management acumen of Toto Wolff, it's easy to see the appeal of a work culture like Mercedes. It's understandable that Lewis Hamilton was drawn to this team and vision to the point of leaving McLaren, even though McLaren had been out-winning Mercedes.

---

73 Pradhan Muthanna, "Lewis Hamilton Sees Long-Term Future At Mercedes, Reveals Michael Schumacher Inspiration," International Business Times, April 23, 2018, https://www. ibtimes.com/lewis-hamilton-sees-long-term-future-mercedes-reveals-michael-schumacher-inspiration-2674382.

74 Andrew Benson, "Formula 1: How Toto Wolff made Mercedes one of sport's greatest teams," BBC Sport, July 9, 2019, https://www.bbc.com/sport/formula1/48911849.

The rest is history. Mercedes and their drivers, including Hamilton, have won every championship since 2014—seven consecutive years. That's a feat even the legendary Ferrari has never achieved, and certainly not McLaren.

So, now when you hear the words Formula 1, don't think of mayo on fries. Think of the first Black F1 driver choosing to join a losing team with a visionary leader, only to be led to near perfection for seven consecutive years by a meditation afficionado named Toto.

THE ONE SKILL TO GET REALLY GOOD AT

"Speech is power: Speech is to persuade, to convert, to compel."
—Ralph Waldo Emerson [75]

I'll let you in on a secret.

The absolutely most important skill to obsess over and aggressively improve is public speaking, and your ability to do this with ease will transform your ability to effectively manage your team.

I know, I know. Usually, people hate public speaking. I happen to be one of the weird freaks who enjoys it. But love it or hate it, you absolutely need to embrace this skill for the following reasons:

1. When you're leading a team meeting, you'll use the power of your speech to motivate, clarify, and to a lesser extent, entertain your team with your unique style of communication.

2. When you're representing your team at cross-department meetings, any contributions you make to the discussion are a direct reflection on

---

75   Ralph Waldo Emerson, Collected Works of Ralph Waldo Emerson, Volume VIII: Letters and Social Aims (Cambridge, MA: Harvard University Press, 2010), 50.

the competency of your team. Speaking well and with conviction will boost the reputation of you and your team.

3. When you're speaking at a larger meeting and your team is present, your team is looking to you to represent them well and inspire them with your clarity of thought and ability to deliver a punch.

4. Being an effective public speaker is one of the surefire ways to impress your boss! And that still matters, big-time, as you are now being evaluated as a leader in the company.

Ultimately, your ability to own the room in a variety of scenarios—from giving a kick-ass TED-style talk at a conference to leading a meeting of disparate professionals like the talented professional you are—is an invaluable component to your and your team's success. Your delivery of a talk or powerful update is a fabulous component to you and your team's brand.

Hate public speaking? Sorry to hear that. Make your peace with it now as you ascend to leadership.

Become a powerful speaker, and you will command the attention and respect of your team and your peers and be a force of nature in bringing your best to represent your team.

The good news? Yes, I promise, there is good news!

Some people are just naturally talented at public speaking, or maybe they spent their coming-of-age years doing things like debate, high school theatre, or other performing arts. Of course, these kinds of leaders will have a natural edge in their public-speaking abilities.

If this wasn't you, don't sweat it (yet—save that for the stage)! Chances are, you're already a fairly strong communicator to have been selected for a management role, so you're already on the right track. You probably also have some degree of emotional intelligence, enough so that your management recognized in you, at a minimum, the potential to connect with people and understand how to motivate them. Both skills translate nicely into public-speaking chops.

And, like many things in life, practice makes perfect (or at least makes it better).

For example, there's a misconception that the everyday Joey can't become a good singer, but of course the vocal muscles can be trained and practiced daily. So, pretty much anyone can sing. Natural ability helps, of course, but it doesn't mean most people can't get to a decent level.

With athletics like basketball, the same rules apply. Obviously, if you're 7 feet tall, you're going to have an advantage. But a really good 5' 8" player could beat the 7-footer. A 5'6" player can even make history. For example, Becky Hammon's relative shortness certainly introduced a natural challenge as she pursued her basketball career. Back in high school, Hammon excelled at the sport, earning her the title of South Dakota Player of the Year in 1994, yet she drew little attention from college recruiters who considered her too small and too slow. Eventually, she drew the attention of an assistant coach who recruited her to Colorado State, where she later flourished as a star player. In 1999, she joined the WNBA, crushing expectations to the point where she earned the nickname Big Shot Becky. [76] After a successful career on the court, Becky next pursued coaching, eventually earning her the historic role of first female assistant coach for the NBA. She also happens to be from my hometown of Rapid City, South Dakota, so I'm basically a stan forever.

To nitpick the whole Practice Makes Perfect concept a little bit, there really isn't a perfect when it comes to public speaking, so let's reword this to say Practice Makes Pretty Darn Good.

What are you waiting for, then? Practice your public speaking, now. Micro-opportunities are everywhere, from asking a question at a company all-hands meeting, to offering to give a toast at your next dinner, to taking the megaphone the next time you protest. And, of course, there's always organizations like Toastmasters to help you hone your talent and creative pursuits like improv classes to get your brain hemispheres fired up.

In addition to straight-up practice, below are a few of my tried-and-true tricks for absolutely owning the room or, in some cases, the Zoom:

1. When you're constructing your next talk, think backwards from the feeling you want to create. From there, design your talking points and messaging to deliver the overall vibe you want to create.

2. Learn the art of using pauses effectively. Watch great speeches by gifted orators to get ideas on how to do this. The pause creates tension, and whatever you say after the pause resolves the tension. It's a very powerful technique!

3. If you're going to absolutely nail any part of your talk, obsess over the first two minutes. Your audience will be evaluating how they feel about you and your message most vividly in the first two minutes.

---

76 Alexandra Wolfe, "Becky Hammon's Big Shot," The Wall Street Journal, April 28, 2017, https://www.wsj.com/articles/becky-hammons-big-shot-1493393914.

4. Identify your ticks and fillers and put them to death! Your "ums," "uhs," "likes," and "ya knows" make you seem unpolished and unsure. Ask your trusted friends to tell you really what they are, and if you can stand it, record yourself talking and listen back. Cringeworthy, but worth it.

5. Learn the theory of power posing and implement it! Biohack your way to success. Note that the science on this is somewhat muddled, but what's the harm in doing it anyway? Try standing straight with your hands on your waist for a couple minutes or puffing your chest and arms out like a gymnast who just landed an Olympic-worthy tumble to get your good vibes flowing before you take the stage next.

6. Understand most audiences have short attention spans, so structure your talk so you are switching gears every few minutes or so to re-engage their brains. For example, you could have a slide where you ask for answers to a question or show a short video instead of delivering the information yourself.

Bottom line is that public speaking is the one thing to obsess over in your own toolkit of talents, and you can get better through some widely accepted simple techniques. And you have to practice and practice some more!

Keep working at it, and you are sure to wow your team at your next meeting and more effectively advocate for them across the organization. Kick ass at public speaking, and your leadership will go to the next level.

chapter 9

BLACK LIVES MATTER: HOW TO DISMANTLE SYSTEMIC RACISM

"The ultimate measure of a person is not where one stands in moments of comfort and convenience, but where one stands in times of challenge and controversy."
—Martin Luther King, Jr.[77]

As a first-time people manager, you may feel like you have the weight of the world on you sometimes. I feel you on that. I take my role as steward of my team and holder of power and influence very seriously, and I often reflect on how I can better use my position to both have a meaningful, prosperous career and make the world a better place. In particular, I have always had a deep sense that part of my purpose on Earth, in this lifetime, is to do what I can to improve racial injustices.

---

77   Martin Luther King, Strength to Love (New York, NY: Harper & Brothers, 1963), 25.

It's a false conclusion to think you can't have and be both—positive business outcomes and racial equity aren't at opposite ends of some kind of life-choices spectrum. They can, and should, coexist as mutually beneficial and interconnected goals.

In the summer of 2019, I fully realized the depth of the reality of systemic racism in the US, and I became filled with a drive to do whatever I could to help address this deep and ugly problem. That summer, I had the opportunity to volunteer inside a maximum-security prison in California.

It was my first time at a maximum-security prison, in any context, and I'm sure it showed. My heart was beating out of my chest as I shuffled through the metal detectors, terrified I would say the wrong thing or fidget in a suspicious-seeming way. I was desperate for a drink of water and determined to cover up my light blue blouse with a coworker's oversized black North Face jacket. I was so intensely anticipating this unique volunteer opportunity that I had completely forgotten that blue was the same color as the prisoners' attire, and thus forbidden as a color for volunteers.

Defy Ventures is a program that matches business leaders with entrepreneurs-in-training (or EITs), the term they prefer to "prisoner" in an effort to destigmatize the scarlet letter of having served time. Volunteers spend the day counseling EITs to give feedback on their business ideas, conduct mock interviews Shark Tank–style, and just spend a few hours connecting and discussing life with each other.

Seared in my mind is the image of the dozens of EITs lined up eagerly awaiting us, as we volunteers walked into the prison gymnasium where the workshops were taking place. Nearly all of them, heartbreakingly, were Black or Latinx—a visceral visual reminder of the effects of systemic racism in our education, economic, and criminal justice systems.

The program encourages the volunteers to post their reflections on social media platforms as well as some professionally produced photos of the workshops and the EITs participating in the sessions. The goal of this practice is to spark intrigue and discussions around criminal justice reform, as well as reduce the stigma of having a criminal history. Unemployment for people in their first years after serving a prison sentence hovers around five times the rate for the general US population and is a major contributing factor to the recidivism rate.[78] Programs like Defy that invest in business skills, self-confidence, and communication skills give the EITs a sense of purpose and hope to defy these statistics (hence the name), and so far, their results have been impressive.[79]

Naturally, I was eager to fulfill the request from the Defy staff, so I wrote a meaningful post on my Facebook page and queued up several photos from the workshops to add the stunning visual element of the EITs enthusiastically participating in the program. But when I uploaded the photos, something happened that startled me.

Facebook's facial-recognition algorithm had attempted to tag one of the EITs that I worked with in the prison as one of my friends. Yes, one of my Black friends. A Black friend who also happens to be an Android engineer.

The Facebook AI couldn't tell the difference between their faces.

Because they looked nothing alike, it almost seemed like the Facebook AI thought, Huh. Incarcerated man. Must be Black. You know who else is Black? That guy. Must be him.

---

78 Steve Horn, "With 27 Percent Unemployment, Jobs Crisis Hits Ex-prisoners the Hardest," Prison Legal News, September 4, 2018, https://www.prisonlegalnews.org/news/2018/sep/4/27-percent-unemployment-jobs-crisis-hits-ex-prisoners-hardest/.
79 Sorenson Impact, "Higher Hope, Lower Recidivism For Defy's Entrepreneurs In Training," Forbes, February 12, 2020, https://www.forbes.com/sites/sorensonimpact/2020/02/04/higher-hope-lower-recidivism-for-defys-eits/?sh=46ffd5fc5c5c.

Of course, this wasn't intentional. No software engineer at Facebook intentionally wrote an algorithm that was less adept at detecting facial structures of Black faces. And nobody wrote any code that translated to "Image of a prisoner: must be Black."

What more likely happened was the programmers working on these systems were not Black themselves, and thus the implicit biases in the programmers' own minds translated into an explicit bias in their collective code base.

But this is what happens in a society and economy where systemic racism runs rampant. It relies on complicated systems of power and access and not on individual attitudes. Because these systems are so ingrained into the fabric of our society, economy, and mental framework, they don't ever really go away.

I ask myself: What really is the difference between a racist algorithm and a racist cop? Are they not both unfortunate and tragic parts of the same system that upholds racism? And, as a member of the leadership cohort that makes hiring, firing, and promotion decisions in the technology sector, what is my role and responsibility in undoing this damage?

The Black Lives Matter movement implores each of us to really dig deep and question if our lives and livelihoods are in alignment with our values. Sadly, many of us in the tech industry are realizing just how complicit our supposedly progressive industry has been when it comes to these matters.

As just one measure of the failure of tech to achieve equity, despite Google's statements in support of diversity in technology, it seems to have made little headway. For example, Black employees make up only two percent of all US Google jobs, two percent of technical ones, and three percent of executive roles. [80] We have to wonder if this appalling disparity was, in part, a contributing factor to the horrifying gaffe when their AI technology tagged two Black people as actual gorillas. [81] Yes, you read that right. In 2015, an incident went viral in which someone realized that Google's facial-recognition software on their phone auto-tagged a photo of two Black people as gorillas.

Holy shit.

So, what is a new people manager to do? How can you leverage your newfound position of power and influence to make a change and live a life that you are proud of, having done your part to dismantle systemic racism within your own industry?

---

80 Ina Fried, "Big Tech's Reckoning on Race," AXIOS, June 12, 2020, https://www.axios.com/big-tech-reckoning-on-race-c03108e5-054c-4bb0-8ea6-df2a0b9230b7.html.
81 Maggie Zhang, "Google Photos Tags Two African-Americans As Gorillas Through Facial Recognition Software," Forbes, July 1, 2015, https://www.forbes.com/sites/mzhang/2015/07/01/google-photos-tags-two-african-americans-as-gorillas-through-facial-recognition-software/?sh=464cb86d713d.

FIRST, PUT ON YOUR OWN OXYGEN MASK

"Self-care is in the little moments—bathing, sweating, washing your hair…
it's in laughing so hard you can barely catch a breath, your lungs expanding
on a morning jog…now more than ever we need to enjoy the quiet within
ourselves."
—Lizzo [82]

Leading a team in these modern times is no joke. Chances are, when you accepted your current role, you had no idea you would be asked to produce business results during a challenging period in world history and a national reckoning with racism in all corners of society.

But here you are, and here we are, together—figuring how to maintain business continuity while navigating what is likely the most daunting challenge of your entire career, and one which will inevitably define your legacy as a leader.

Let me start by giving you the permission to breathe and acknowledge that so much is being asked of you right now, and you're not always going to get it right.

That's okay.

As managers, we wear many hats. We function as stewards of our employees' well-being, we represent their needs to other departments and our own leadership, and we provide emotional presence, warmth, and compassion for each employee's unique circumstance and ability.

We also know how much our coaching and approach affect our employees' well-being, quality of life, and ability to grow professionally and take care

---

82   Hannah-Rose Yee, "Lizzo's best quotes on body positivity, self-care and empowerment," Stylist, accessed May 20, 2021, https://www.stylist.co.uk/entertainment/celebrity/lizzo-best-quotes-self-love-body-positivity-empowerment/263004.

of their families. Chances are, you take this responsibility very seriously in the best of times and even more seriously in the worst of times.

It's. Okay. To. Breathe.

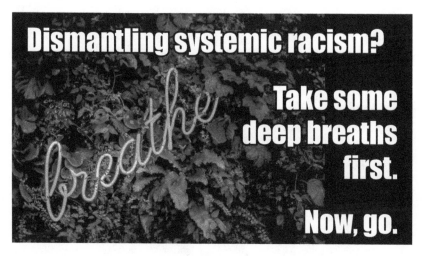

Breathe in, breathe out. This is a marathon, not a sprint, and you are needed in the long run!

Once you've caught your breath, take a moment and reflect on how much power and influence you have in your workplace and in your industry. Quality front-line managers are one of the most valuable assets in any company, and your contributions and leadership at this moment in history are of serious consequence.

Let me not mince words. You are in one of the most viable positions at this moment to be an agent of change to address systemic racism in your industry and space. You are in your role because your company leadership trusts you to lead the day-to-day, and your input and impact are magnified at this moment.

Do not squander it.

So, what kind of change is needed?

In your heart, if you truly believe that talent is equally distributed across all races but you don't see all races reflected at all levels in your workplace and industry, you know we have a problem. And this problem is just as ugly and deep as what we've seen playing out in the streets of the US these past years when it comes to police violence on Black and brown citizens.

CAN THIS BE THE INFLECTION POINT?

"I'm no longer accepting the things I cannot change…I'm changing the things I cannot accept."
—Attributed to Angela Davis

To move the needle forward, we're all going to have to change hearts, minds, and outcomes, but first it's important to look inward. All of us, no matter our position or background, are part of the social and institutional fabric that enables systemic racism. The ongoing legacy of slavery has created and continues to facilitate generational wealth divides and the brutal nature of cyclical poverty. There are many ways to attempt to measure how widespread and pervasive these issues are. A study in the Boston area recently found that the net worth of the average Black family was quite literally $8, in contrast with the average for white families at $247,000. [83]

The past few years seem to indicate we are in the middle of the most significant civil rights uprising in modern times, and many Americans are cautiously optimistic that we are at a turning point with racial justice in the United States, as am I.

---

83   Selena Hill, "Report: Blacks in Boston Have a Median Net Worth of $8, Whites Have $247K," *Black Enterprise*, December 13, 2017, https://www.blackenterprise.com/blacks-boston-median-net-worth-8/.

In late May 2020, George Floyd's horrific murder by a police officer stirred something deep within most Americans, at a time when emotions were already raw from economic depression, social isolation, and our worst fears about struggling to breathe due to the coronavirus. [84]

But why?

We know intellectually that these things happen all the time. But, in other more recent viral incidents of police killing citizens, they involve gunfire, which is quick, reactive, and in part the product of an amped-up, adrenaline-fueled situation. While equally unacceptable, it's easier to somehow explain it away by blaming unconscious bias, lack of training, or implicit racial profiling.

It seems that as a society, we can somehow rationalize the horror by empathizing with a frightened, reactive cop being somehow afraid for their life in a high-stress situation and making a bad judgement call as a result of their bias.

But, as we all know, George Floyd's death is different. Watching officers kneel on his neck while he called out for his mother sickened us and urged us to examine our hearts and worldview. It has called us to acknowledge and begin the work to cast out the other kind of racism deeply rooted in our guts—the kind that explains away snap judgements based on race persistent in our society.

In the 1960s, another turning point in respect to civil rights, a large number of Americans had more traditionally racist viewpoints. [85] Racism was a lot easier to define and confront in 1963, because it was a good litmus test

84   Alex Altman, "Why The Killing of George Floyd Sparked an American Uprising," TIME, June 4, 2020, https://time.com/5847967/george-floyd-protests-trump/.
85   Charles Kenny, "The data are in: Young people are increasingly less racist than old people," Quartz, May 24, 2017, https://qz.com/983016/the-data-are-in-young-people-are-definitely-less-racist-than-old-people/.

of whether you thought there should be separate water fountains or that interracial marriage should be legal. Back then, being for equality simply meant that you didn't think outright discrimination was acceptable.

You would be more hard-pressed nowadays to find anyone openly admitting they have these views, which is unquestionable progress in the battle towards equality.

But now we are facing a sneakier enemy, and that, of course, is systemic racism. Systemic racism is much harder to confront because it's structured into every aspect of American life. There's no one law, election, or individual who is responsible for it.

Systematic racism creates the following juxtaposition: Although "separate but equal" is no longer the law of the land, American schools are actually more segregated today than in 1968.[86] The problem is complex and merits a book of its own, but there are certainly some contributing factors. Economic segregation, income and wealth inequality, and mass incarceration are just some of the issues in the past 50 years that have perpetuated the vicious cycle.

We simply must address each of these issues as a comprehensive part of the current uprising.

In a more overtly racist society, like that of the US in the 1960s, it may have felt like enough to consciously reject outright discrimination and segregation—and at that time, it would have been more radical, more daring, and anti-racist to do so.

But this time, it's different. We are facing a much different beast that lurks in every corner of our society and convinces us that if we believe that all are created equal in our hearts, then that is enough.

---

86 Valerie Strauss, "Report: Public Schools More Segregated Now Than 40 Years Ago," the Washington Post, August 29, 2013, https://www.washingtonpost.com/news/answer-sheet/wp/2013/08/29/report-public-schools-more-segregated-now-than-40-years-ago/.

It's not enough.

This moment demands us to dig deep to understand just how much systematic racism has gripped our hearts and minds.

HERE'S HOW WE GET THERE

"I tell law students…if you are going to be a lawyer and just practice your profession, you have a skill—very much like a plumber. But if you want to be a true professional, you will do something outside yourself…something that makes life a little better for people less fortunate than you."
—Ruth Bader Ginsburg [87]

Dismantling systemic racism in our respective workplaces is going to be hard. But we have to start somewhere, and now that you're in a position of power and influence, your legacy in moving the arc of history towards justice is amplified.

So, what can you do within the scope of your career as a people manager?

1. **Take ownership of your recruiting process.** The most immediately impactful way to fight systemic racism is to ensure you take your power as a hiring manager very seriously when it comes to ensuring there is widespread and equal access to opportunities on your team and at your company, as we've covered in previous chapters. You simply must be an active participant in your recruiting process and be hands-on in diversifying the pipeline and not place this expectation solely on your recruiting team.

---

87   Kathleen J. Sullivan, "U.S. Supreme Court Justice Ruth Bader Ginsburg talks about a meaningful life," Stanford, February 6, 2017, https://news.stanford.edu/2017/02/06/supreme-court-associate-justice-ginsburg-talks-meaningful-life/.

2. **Advocate to end employee referral bonuses.** Employee referrals are a common tactic to hire within existing employer networks. The only problem is that they create an incentive for employees to refer their friends, and when you've already got a diversity problem, this will compound it. Furthermore, the sheer size of some bonuses for technical roles exacerbates income inequalities already present in the socio-economic strata of your employee population. Does an engineer really need an extra $10k to refer another software engineer?

3. **Invest in internal pipelines of talent.** You should also work to ensure there are pipelines and coaching programs internally from lower-barrier-to-entry roles to higher-barrier-to-entry roles and ensure you are working with managers to source from these teams. A great example in most software companies is your support population—usually quite remarkably more diverse than other customer-facing roles, and yet this group is often overlooked as a talent pool to coach into higher paid or more technical roles. However, the demands of a support role inevitably develop the core fundamentals—deep product knowledge, ability to multitask, sharp customer-facing communication, and ability to empathize—that make a great support agent a competitive candidate for other career paths. If this applies to you, don't overlook your support team population when looking for your next great hire, and ensure they are coached and encouraged to apply for other roles.

4. **Insist on fair and by-the-book hiring processes for new roles.** Do not create roles for single individuals, and do interview outside your internal candidates for these roles, period. This practice is common in the tech industry and is harmful for diversity, because it underscores existing social and professional networks in your company and does not provide a fair process for all candidates to apply and be considered. If you see this happening, insist that job descriptions are written and posted, and that all internal candidates are aware of the opportunity at a minimum.

5. **Advocate for profit sharing and equity grants at every level.** Transgenerational wealth is one of the biggest factors that aggravates inequality and prevents every American from having equal opportunity to succeed. Beyond paying a reasonable salary that ensures your team generally doesn't have to worry about money, work with your leadership team to compensate via equity (as well as education on how equity over time generates wealth). Does your employee population understand how the equity compensation package can transform into compounding wealth? If your employees didn't grow up in a household where home ownership, the stock market, and other financial instruments beyond cash income were discussed, you may need to do the heavy lifting here to empower and educate with this type of financial literacy.

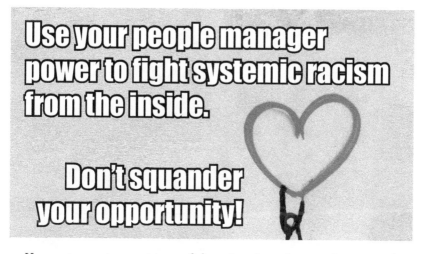

You are in a unique position to fight racism through your role as a people manager. Don't squander it!

And finally, I want to circle back to the importance of always taking care of your own mental and physical health, not only to keep yourself energized for the long term but also to serve as an example of investing in self-care during these trying times.

We have a lot of work ahead of us, and it's going to take a lot of time, energy, passion, and teamwork to get it all done, over a long period of time. Do not burn yourself out. Give yourself permission to relax, make mistakes and learn from them, and trust in your ability to still provide leadership to your team even when you're not feeling your best.

We can do this!

chapter 10

TRICKY STUFF

"It is no use saying, 'we are doing our best.' You have to succeed in doing what is necessary."
—Winston Churchill[88]

In this chapter, we're going to go over how to handle some of the yucky stuff, like employee compensation dissatisfaction, sexual harassment issues, interteam conflicts, and the absolute worst of them all, terminating an employee.

These unpleasant topics are nowhere near fun, but they are necessary to ace with the same badassery you've applied to responsibilities in your job that are significantly more fun, such as planning a team-building activity.

Read on to see how you do it.

---

88   Robert Rhodes James, ed., Churchill Speaks: Collected Speeches in Peace and War, 1897-1967 (Barnes & Noble, 1998).

CASH RULES EVERYTHING AROUND ME

"I can't wait to be a people manager so I can negotiate compensation packages with my team members and often feel like I'm disappointing them!"
—said no one ever

It's time to get down to it and discuss cold, hard cash.

Let's be real. There are three things in life that are most always true. Everyone secretly loves trash TV, Paul Rudd doesn't age, and nobody is happy with the amount of money they're making.

Luckily, only one of these is really your problem in your new role. But it is a problem nonetheless!

As a front-line manager, you will be the one having the down-to-business conversations with your direct reports about their compensation. You are a representative arm of your company's bottom line, and it is your responsibility to be prudent with that.

These conversations can be some of the most uncomfortable conversations, as they can truly be an emotional landmine. It's almost impossible to pay your team what they think they should be making. Nearly everyone has some sort of complicated and emotional relationship with money or to some degree measures their self-worth by their W2 statement (they shouldn't, but you know that this is true).

Conversations about compensation are the situations when you often have to really put on your objective hat and try to remain as detached as possible. This is a time where you'll have to reel your empathy back and empower yourself to act as a neutral, transactional agent of your finance department.

This is super tough, but you need to simultaneously manage up and down. That is to say, you will experience downward pressure from your management chain to push wages down, while at the same time you will experience upward pressure from your direct reports to push wages up as much as you can.

At the end of the day, you are equally accountable to your team members to negotiate as high a compensation package as you can for them as you are to your company's leadership and shareholders to keep operating costs down so you can stay solvent and agile.

You will be evaluated on your ability to delicately balance these two opposing forces without getting crushed, as both groups need to feel like you're on their team. Your management needs to feel you are carrying the best interests of the company, and your team will need to feel you are fighting and advocating for them. Pay or compensation outcomes are some of the most easily measurable ways to show results in both. It's not easy!

The conversations you will have concerning pay are also difficult because they deal directly with asking for money, which can be very difficult for everyone involved. It is really uncomfortable asking for money.

Like I said, pay conversations are not anyone's favorite.

So, where is the room where it happens? As a first-time manager, you'll need to figure this out soon, although you shouldn't expect to get a complete picture of how these decisions are made for a while.

Compensation can also vary widely based on your industry, market conditions, company health and trajectory, and so on. Typically, most firms have one or two predesignated review cycles annually where comp adjustments take place (although there are some exceptions, discussed later). This is useful to know because, as mentioned before, comp conversations are almost always difficult and require a lot of thoughtfulness.

Without a prescribed time to address these conversations, it could be an ongoing pain point and recurring topic of conversation during one-on-ones with your team, which can impede work getting done. That said, expect your team to bring up comp whenever they want and always be prepared to have talking points ready when they do.

In fact, you probably won't have direct control over comp levels and will be working in tandem with your manager, HR, finance, and possibly a management team to make compensation decisions, so it's not exactly like you get promoted to management and suddenly you can make executive decisions about compensation.

It also could be that you have very little control over compensation bands at all, as it is likely that someone determined a compensation strategy well before you got into your management position. This isn't to say that you can't change things, but you'll have to first prove yourself as a manager to be able to make a meaningful difference in compensation philosophy or individual compensation decisions at your firm or company.

Good luck marching into your boss's office (or aggressively pressing Start Video on your Zoom meeting, as the case may be) and demanding raises for your team before you've proven yourself as a competent and trustworthy steward of company finances. It just ain't gonna work this way, and even if it did, what would you base it on? Have you done the market research, competitive analysis, and P&L (profit and loss) analysis to make a meaningful recommendation for compensation bands for your team's expertise?

Probably not. So, get used to not being able to push the needle much, at least in the early part of your management career.

Conversations around compensation, especially during predetermined review cycles, are tough. You will say no more than you will say yes. Get used to it!

The good news: Because of your relatively new tenure in having these types of conversations, your manager will most likely support the hell out of you in your first few rounds of compensation conversations. If you can't lean on them, find another manager or go to HR. Support and guidance are crucial during this period for you to succeed, so don't be afraid to ask for help.

It's going to be super important for you to appear both credible to your team members in being able to make meaningful changes and credible to your upper-management chain in being able to navigate those conversations effectively, eventually. Also, as a new manager, your employees might think they can get more out of you given your relative inexperience, so prepare to be pushed as far as possible in your first round of this.

One thing to keep in mind is that you really need to be mindful and deliberate in your word choice during these conversations, especially if you were previously a peer to your team members before your promotion. You need to be able to detach yourself, as you'll essentially be an acting representative of your company during this time. Get comfortable saying phrases like these:

"I understand you're disappointed, but there is no wiggle room for more."

"I can't promise a raise the next cycle."

"The bonus decision is final."

And this should be obvious, but you'll want to avoid phrases like the following:

"I agree it's so unfair how little you make compared to Jimmy!"

"If you work even harder this year, I bet you can get a promotion in June!"

"I had no say in these compensation decisions; it's really out of my hands."

Bottom line: Boss the eff up and handle these conversations with grace, directness, and the appropriate level of emotional detachment to not get wrapped up in your employees' emotional relationship with money, titles, etc. You are not ultimately responsible for their happiness, and that includes their satisfaction with their salary.

You are a trusted coach and mentor to help them unlock their own achievements and reach their goals. You have a job to do. So, get it done.

MANAGING IN THE #METOO ERA

"I have waited tables in restaurants. I have ridden the subway. I have walked the streets in New York City. And this kind of language is not new…I have tossed men out of bars that have used language like Mr. Yoho's, and I have encountered this type of harassment riding the subway in New York City. This is not new. And that is the problem."
—Alexandra Ocasio-Cortez, in response to comments made by Ted Yoho, who allegedly directed vulgar insults at her [89]

In 2017, the exposure of widespread sexual harassment and abuse allegations against film producer Harvey Weinstein seemed to release a pressure valve in the hearts of women around the world, when the #MeToo hashtag went viral on Twitter and other platforms. The hashtag was used to show just how widespread sexual harassment is, and invited women to share their stories of the abuse of power by using the hashtag. [90]

Although this was the most viral, widespread use of the phrase heard 'round the internet, the phrase "Me Too" was initially used in this context on social media in 2006, on Myspace, by sexual harassment survivor and activist Tarana Burke. [91]

The #MeToo movement, over the past few years, has illuminated the deeply rooted injustices that many women face in the workplace. And while sexual harassment is only one of those, it's one that can be the most dam-

---

89   Allan Smith, "AOC admonishes GOP congressman in fiery speech: 'I am someone's daughter,'" NBC News, July 23, 2020, https://www.nbcnews.com/politics/congress/aoc-admonishes-gop-congressman-fiery-speech-i-am-someone-s-n1234699.

90   "#MeToo: Harvey Weinstein case moves thousands to tell their stories of abuse, break silence," the Washington Post, October 16, 2017, https://www.washingtonpost.com/news/morning-mix/wp/2017/10/16/me-too-alyssa-milano-urged-assault-victims-to-tweet-in-solidarity-the-response-was-massive/.

91   Chris Snyder and Linette Lopez, "Tarana Burke on wy she created the #MeToo movement – and where it's headed," Business Insider, December 13, 2017, https://www.businessinsider.com/how-the-metoo-movement-started-where-its-headed-tarana-burke-time-person-of-year-women-2017-12.

aging. Studies suggest that 81 percent of women-identifying people experience sexual harassment in their lifetime in general, and 38 percent of them report it having happened in the workplaces. [92]

Of course, sexual harassment doesn't just apply to women, although women certainly experience the majority of it. Harassment of any kind is a big deal and can permanently damage someone's career and mental health. It can also put your company in serious legal jeopardy.

As a manager, you are now not only an extension and official representative of your company's HR policies, but you're also a leader in helping define what those policies are. Like it or not, you're now in a position of management where you are entrusted to handle sensitive issues like sexual harassment, and now more than ever, you do have the ability to create positive change from your new position of power.

To be more specific, there are possibly two main situations you'll encounter. One is that someone you manage is accused of sexual harassment. The second is where someone you manage comes forward as having experienced sexual harassment. Both situations could involve another coworker, a customer, a vendor, or a partner.

Yuck. Big Yuck.

If either of these situations occurs, get help from your HR partner immediately. Like, yesterday.

You are dealing with a complex legal matter that is frankly beyond your scope, and you do not need to be a hero right now. Follow the advice of

---

92   Rhitu Chatterjee, "A New Survey Finds 81 Percent Of Women Have Experienced
       Sexual Harassment," NPR, February 21, 2018, https://www.npr.org/sections/thetwo-
       way/2018/02/21/587671849/a-new-survey-finds-eighty-percent-of-women-have-experienced-
       sexual-harassment.

your HR and legal team's direction to the T and execute on any investigations or directives precisely.

But, as they say, an ounce of prevention is worth a pound of cure. So, let's wind back the clock to what you can and should do to prevent anything like the previous scenarios taking place.

Priority number one: Work with your manager and HR teams to prioritize any mandatory training you'll need to have completed. These certification requirements vary by state and are usually designed to protect your employer from lawsuits. Frankly, they're the bare minimum to reduce risk and make sure you're going to be fully compliant from a legal standpoint. That said, the law is the law and it's something you'll need to know intimately so you can protect yourself, protect your team, and protect your company and shareholders from risk. Alongside any regulatory topics you'll need to know, you should also know your company-specific policies and channels for reporting issues. Learn who your HR partners are in addressing issues, like sexual harassment.

Priority number two: Develop trust with your team so you can have a frank dialogue about sexual-harassment issues if and when they arise. If your team doesn't feel comfortable raising issues or concerns with you, it's possible they'll sweep issues under the rug or go above you when problems arise. Have an open conversation with your team and individually about how important it is that everyone feels safe and comfortable at work and that your door is always open to talk about issues that prevent that from taking place.

Priority number three: Educate yourself and others about gender bias in the workplace. This topic deserves a book of its own, but you should be familiar with some of the basics. Gender bias can take many forms, including subtle differences in how different genders are recruited, hired, coached, promoted, and ultimately judged at all levels in an organization across all industries. Much like racial bias, gender bias is pervasive and systemic, and it will likely take generations of focused effort to overcome.[93]

As just one illustration, the University of Exeter recently examined just how prevalent discrimination towards women in the workplace is. In one study, they found that hiring managers who had been given identical descriptions of two prospective employees, one male and one female, had rated the male higher than the female and recommended a starting salary 8 percent higher for the male candidate.[94]

Workplaces and teams with severe gender bias are ripe environments for sexual harassment because the power dynamic is already so imbalanced. Therefore, focusing on the subtler steps to tackle and root out gender bias is like "a stitch in time saves nine" when it comes to preventing harassment.

No offense to anyone actually named Brad!

The crux of the matter is this: Sexual harassment is just about the most serious thing you will (hopefully never) deal with as a people manager,

---

93 John Anderer, "Workplace Gender Bias is Very Much Alive and Well and This is Why," Ladders, June 30, 2020, https://www.theladders.com/career-advice/workplace-gender-bias-is-very-much-alive-and-well-and-this-is-why.

94 "Gender bias kept alive by people who think it's dead," University of Exeter, June 24, 2020, https://www.exeter.ac.uk/news/homepage/title_802676_en.html.

but if you do, get help immediately. Document, listen, be objective, and understand that this is a much bigger problem than we think, so take it seriously from the get-go.

INTERTEAM CONFLICTS

"I wish we could all get along like we used to in middle school. I wish I could bake a cake filled with rainbows and smiles and everyone would eat and be happy."
—*Crying Girl, Mean Girls*[95]

Management would be so easy if it weren't for all the managing.

Humans in group settings inevitably have interpersonal conflict. It's just our nature as humanoids. I mean, have you ever seen the Real Housewives franchise?

You and your team are no exception.

Conflict in and of itself isn't a bad thing. In fact, one of the litmus tests of a healthy team vibe is the sense of psychological safety that encourages productive creative conflict. Creative conflict is unique and distinguishable from interpersonal conflict, as it is the hivemind you've built working as designed. Each person offers a unique perspective and life experience, and through the process and iteration of brainstorming, feedback, and compromise, innovation is likely to happen. That's a good thing.

But interpersonal conflict is a different beast.

It is unrealistic to expect that your entire team will get along fabulously, or even necessarily like each other on a personal level. Plus, it's not your job

---

95   Mean Girls, dir. Mark Waters, 2004, Paramount Pictures, 97 mins.

to manage their emotions about each other. Each employee is responsible for handling themselves professionally and with maturity in the workplace. For that reason, don't fixate on this if you can obviously tell that a couple of your team members aren't meshing, unless it's at the point where it's causing dysfunction, discrimination, and/or abuse.

Also, if you get too involved with interpersonal conflict, it may create even more problems, since your team now has the expectation that you will play counselor to them. Then, when the next conflict inevitably arises, you've set a precedent that you can come in and help them resolve it.

But are you ready to get even deeper? If your personality is fundamentally a fixer or avoidant type, these interpersonal conflicts may eat at you and could ultimately break you as a manager.

For this and many other reasons, therapy and/or coaching is your friend. Understanding what triggers conflict for you as a result of your childhood or any other life experiences is critical to being empowered to handle conflicts in your team.

Now, what do you actually do when these conflicts arise?

Most of the time, nothing. You may not even know about these conflicts, as they could well be happening behind the scenes and your team members are working these out on their own. That's certainly the idea and is more common with employees that have a few years of professional experience under their belt.

However, if your team members bring it to your attention, you do need to at least respond to it.

Again, your responsibility here isn't necessarily to fix it, but to empower your individual team members to resolve it on their own or to coach them on how to peacefully coexist with it (especially if they are more junior in their careers, they won't necessarily have gained this skill).

Team conflict got you spun up in a tizzy? Turn inward to understand your own conflict response originated in childhood.

Conflict on your team often stirs up unconscious feelings from how conflict affected you in childhood. Learn how your triggers and reactions are activated by team conflict, and you'll be better positioned to navigate this.

You might be wondering if something is serious enough to take to HR, and frankly this is where you'll have to use your best judgement. Of course, your team is free to go to HR whenever they want; you are not a gatekeeper to this resource. But if the conflict is so severe or dysfunctional that it is affecting the ability of your team to function or starts to resemble harassment, then you should consider bringing in an HR representative to guide you. However, for most interpersonal conflicts, the damage is frustrating but not so severe that HR is required to intervene.

So, assuming you haven't brought in HR, you might be wondering, Okay, how do I fix this myself?

As an empathetic and solution-oriented leader, the temptation to drive the conflict towards resolution will always be there, but keep in mind that in the future, your team members won't necessarily have a manager who is so involved with these. By fixing it for them this time, you may not be teaching them the skills they need to thrive in future stages of their careers.

That being said, following are a couple examples of interteam conflict and how I handled it.

EXAMPLE 1: FRIENDLY COMPETITION GONE TOXIC

I took over as manager for a fairly junior technical team during their busiest season, and I could almost immediately feel some bad vibes between two members of the team, Cecilia and Mohammed, who were clearly two highly talented and spirited individuals. The outgoing manager mentioned that there was some backstory: The two had been finalists for a promotion that neither of them actually got. But Mohammed had made it one round beyond Cecilia, which enraged her. The outgoing manager, when doing our handoff, indicated that for both individuals in question, this was their second year out of college, and they were both relatively new to the industry.

For the first few weeks, I didn't inquire about or acknowledge the rivalry, wondering if with a fresh start of the year and new goals for the team, they would outgrow it. But a month or so into the new job, Cecilia mentioned to me that she was struggling with Mohammed on a personal level. I asked her if she could tell me more about it, trying to stay neutral and approaching it from a place of curiosity.

Cecilia then rattled off a long list of nitpicks, many of them simply personality quirks that rubbed her the wrong way. Then she made some more substantial complaints about his performance that seemed particularly frustrating to her, given that he had advanced one round further than she had for the promotion. The first few times she mentioned this conflict, I simply took notes, nodded, and tried to empathize without making judgement or providing suggestions.

For his part, Mohammed never once brought up the conflict to me personally, but I did observe that he often discussed his career with unrealistic expectations, believing he was several levels above where he was. However, he was an articulate and polished communicator and carried himself with a bit more professionalism than Cecilia, so I suspected this is why he had advanced further than she had in the promotion cycle at play.

Meanwhile, my coaching with Cecilia took a turn when she expressed interest in pursuing a different career path. Our one-on-ones evolved from discussing the work itself to thoughtfully crafting a strategic approach to getting her ready for a promotion to another department. I made introductions to key leaders in that department, encouraged her to take on projects that more closely emulated her desired career path, and delivered needed feedback about professionalism in the workplace to assist her with the perception about her abilities.

When she brought up her struggles with Mohammed, I would simply steer her to her own career and encourage her to stay motivated by the conflict. I knew that if she focused on pursuing her own dreams and ambitions, she would quickly level up. Essentially, I asked her to trust the process, and to trust me. I could clearly see her potential and was committed to working with her to get her there. I also challenged her to use the opportunity to work on her own mental abilities to thrive in a workplace despite interpersonal conflict (because that never really goes away). So, rather than fixating on resolving it now, I suggested she focus on developing the skills needed to succeed despite it.

On Mohammed's part, I started to get complaints from other team members about incomplete work. Multiple times in our one-on-ones, he complained about his salary and not getting a promotion. It was quite frustrating, especially considering he had so much potential and I could see he was squandering it. My Spidey senses were activated; thus, I started documenting these complaints and delivered feedback about missed expectations. Unfortunately, he always had an excuse.

The final straw was when he didn't show for his performance review. From there, I alerted HR and began the process of a PIP (Performance Improvement Plan), and he resigned soon after.

Six months later, Cecilia was offered a role on the team and department she had been pursuing, and today, she is thriving.

I was so proud to see someone who had worked so hard, put in the time, and had overcome a tough work situation end up getting a well-deserved promotion and fast-tracked to a career path she felt really excited about.

EXAMPLE 2: SOMETIMES DOING NOTHING IS EVERYTHING

David's and Nicole's backgrounds couldn't have been more different. That was intentional when I hired them both in an effort to diversify the perspectives of the team. David had immigrated to the United States a few years previously from Mexico. While bright, ambitious, and hardworking, he did not have a background specific to the industry in which we worked. Nicole had years of experience in the field and very much understood the pain points and lifestyle of the customers we served.

David was married with two small children in a suburb, and Nicole was single and living with a roommate in a major urban center. Nicole hadn't traveled much outside of her community through the years and did not have strong business communications skills. David preferred not to travel unless necessary, and Nicole jumped at the opportunity to travel as much as possible.

For the most part, David and Nicole worked together swimmingly when they were paired together on projects. Nicole contributed her deep industry knowledge, and David took that knowledge and translated it into beautifully crafted presentations and other deliverables. Outside observers noted that the combination of their skill sets and background seemed optimal, and customers loved working with them.

One day, David and Nicole were assigned to create a major project together over a six-week period for an upcoming sales meeting. They were given guidelines and overall vision for the finished product, and then left to their own devices to work on it together and deliver it to the entire team as a partnership. And they did—six weeks later, they unveiled the finished product, and it blew everyone's mind.

Privately, David complained that Nicole had not done much of the work. He said he had done the majority of the heavy lifting and only relied on Nicole for some industry knowledge and minor contributions. Nicole had also insisted on being the one to walk through the product demonstration, which gave the perception to many leaders in the company that Nicole had played the leading role in completing the work.

Although I suspected David's complaint was valid based on what I knew about the difference in their abilities, as well as Nicole's love of the spotlight, I asked David if he had expressed any of this to Nicole. He said that he hadn't. I asked why, and he said he didn't want to create any friction.

Nicole never mentioned anything to me about the incident, but we had already talked several times about the need for her to continue developing skills in business communications and organization—and she always wholeheartedly agreed. We had even established a system where she would occasionally send me her customer emails to critique and give feedback for her learning. She was making progress, slowly, with this help. She understood that this would be a critical skill to continue progressing in going forward.

For David's part, I told him that unless he was able to discuss this with Nicole directly, there wasn't much I could or would do. But I also reiterated that I did know him to be an excellent contributor, resourceful, and with tremendous potential in the company. I accepted his complaint and acknowledged that if it had happened as he described, it was probably annoying but would likely happen again, if not with Nicole, then with other coworkers. Therefore, it wouldn't serve him to dwell on this situation, but we could work with him on developing more confidence in taking credit for his contributions.

I never did get another complaint like this for Nicole, so I believed it was a one-off interpersonal issue that didn't require any further investigation. Both Nicole and I were aligned that developing the skills we outlined together were important for her to continue to advance. She was self-aware of her strengths and weaknesses.

So, this is an example of where I did pretty much nothing. There were no egregious violations and the complaint about Nicole was probably valid, but not one that I ever got again about her work. Nicole also understood where she stood as a contributor and did not have an expectation for a promotion until she had gained the skills we outlined. David understood that part of the issue is his ability to express confidence in owning his accomplishments, and that would be important moving forward for him to grow.

Two years later, they've both advanced to the next level and have gotten new, fancier titles. And they get along just fine and are now senior members of the team and work together frequently to mentor and coach newer members.

Sometimes doing nothing except facilitating reflection behind the scenes with your team members (so next time they won't need you) is actually doing everything.

MISDEMEANORS VERSUS FELONIES: HR IS YOUR FRIEND

"The things that go unsaid are often the things that eat at you."
—*Celeste Ng*[96]

Blatant lies on expense reports.

Getting so drunk during a company function that an ambulance was called.

Inappropriately touching a customer.

Have you started to vomit in your mouth yet?

Unfortunately, you will probably encounter at least a handful of times in your management career a situation in which someone who reports to you does something so egregious or out of line that you'll need to take action, in the HR sense of the word. Let's revisit the difference between felonies and misdemeanors in the workplace. Minor gaffes (misdemeanors) can be corrected with coaching and redirection. Major missteps (felonies), on the other hand, are the ones that that are clearly unacceptable, dangerous, illegal, or otherwise problematic to the point where direct and immediate action is needed.

Although this analogy and distinction of misdemeanors versus felonies isn't quite the best way to ascribe the differences between workplace inci-

---

96   Celeste Ng, "A Conversation with Celeste Ng, Author of Everything I Never Told You," Everything I Never Told You (New York, NY: Penguin Books, 2015), 307.

dents, it serves its purpose. Misdemeanors are posting a joke in Slack that is off-color and requires a corrective conversation about Slack etiquette. Felonies are sharing company trade secrets with competitors.

The good news here, actually the great news, is that this is exactly the situation where your HR department is your friend. Across the tech landscape, there is a slew and variety of opinions on how HR hurts and helps people in their roles, and while clearly there is a mixed bag of emotions about these departments in general, I can say from personal experience that in almost every tough disciplinary situation, I wished I had engaged HR much earlier.

When you're dealing with a situation where you're almost sure you'll need to either enact disciplinary action, put your employee on a PIP, or remove them from the workplace altogether, you need to 100 percent defer to the legal advice of your designated HR representative. In fact, it is in your best interest to start engaging them as soon as your Spidey senses are activated, and it's good to start documenting situations as they occur, just to protect yourself and your company if things do go, let's say, sideways.

When it comes to major performance issues, HR. Is. Your. Friend.

Here are some tips to prevent and cope with the felonies if they happen:

1. Give gentle but firm reminders before company events about professionalism. I will usually send an email to my team before any sort of event that involves alcohol reminding them of the basics:

   a. This is a work event, so act accordingly.

   b. Friendly reminder that hard alcohol takes longer to metabolize.

   c. Drink plenty of water.

   d. If you see someone who has had too much to drink, pull them or me aside and let's intervene before something bad happens.

   e. Nothing good happens after midnight.

2. Screenshot and save any and all evidence that comes across your desk and any corrective messaging you've provided. If things get ugly, you'll want documentation that any individual in question was reprimanded and directed towards corrective actions, even when things seem minor at first.

3. Be paranoid about system access that your team has, and if things go south quickly, know how to act immediately to shut off any internal systems they have access to: customer information, customer environments, internal communications systems like Slack or email, etc. It's happened a time or two where someone does destructive work on their company's assets on their way out. Not pretty.

If the absolute worst-case scenario happens—and it will at some point in your career—in which you have to make the decision to fire an employee, I am here to tell you that you will get through it. It is not a pleasant experience, and it will feel just awful. HR and legal are your best friends. Follow their guidance to the book.

It will probably go down something like this. In preparation, you should sync with your HR and IT departments to coordinate when systems and access (like badges) will be turned off. You will deliver the message in a one-on-one meeting that you've set up with the employee, most likely on a Friday towards the end of the day. It will be in person, if possible, but it can be done over Zoom, etc. if necessary. You will say something like, "There's no easy way to say this, but this is your last day at Acme, Inc. because of your performance. Thank you for your time and contributions, and best of luck to you."

(Make sure to have some Kleenex handy.)

Then, you will leave the room and HR will take it from there, including logistics, such as the return of company property, offboarding from benefits, and last paycheck.

Double-check with your IT and security department that the employee no longer has access to your internal systems, company email, corporate social media pages, etc. If an email redirect or transfer of cloud-based documents to you makes sense, ensure that is done, because you do have to provide continuity with whatever work projects are in flight.

After the deed is done, you might feel like throwing up. But you're not quite in the clear yet.

Next, you will need to notify the rest of the team about the departure of the person.

Ensure you respect the person's privacy and dignity by keeping your discussions around what happened at a high level and strongly communicate that you wish the person nothing but the best of luck with future endeavors— stay classy! Don't ever communicate to the team about the firing versus quitting—keep it vague.

Below is a sample email to start with:

> *Subject: Team Update*
>
> *Body: Good morning, team. Wanted to let you know right away that as of this morning, Roger Stonewall is no longer with Acme, Inc. We thank him for his years of contributions and wish him the best of luck in the future.*
>
> *If you have been working directly with Roger on a project, please let me know immediately so we can determine another resource and next step.*

Then, you'll need to act quickly to reassign Roger's work (though ideally, you already have some sort of transition plan in mind prior to the termination date), as well as mentally prepare to be peppered with questions about what happened. You'll do best by staying detached but direct and providing ambiguous answers like, "It didn't work out, unfortunately."

Trust me, the team will know what happened in the subtext of your responses and to some degree could feel spooked that this could happen to them. These feelings may also be intermingled with a sense of relief, because it's usually crystal clear to the remaining team when someone isn't performing up to snuff or is causing interpersonal issues in the group.

For both reasons, it is helpful to reassure the remaining team that you continue to be invested in their growth, are here as a supportive leader, and are being totally transparent with them regularly about their strengths and areas of opportunity.

And make sure that that is always true!

Getting fired for performance issues (i.e., not a one-off, out-of-character, flagrant, fireable offense) should never come as a surprise to the individual, or even the team around them, if you are doing your job and delivering regular, actionable feedback and giving your team a realistic reflection of where they stand.

Are you freaked? Don't be.

Most of your employees won't have those kinds of issues. Sometimes there will be an employee who agrees to move on after you both determine the role isn't a good fit. That's great when that happens! The role you've played to move them forward into the next phase of their career is extremely valuable.

But, for that 1 percent of the time you do have to separate someone, it will be brutal. Just know that you'll get through it and come out the other side a more compassionate and decisive leader.

Your former employee will eventually move on just fine, too, but that's going to be up to them. You can't spend too much time fretting over it—you've got a whole remaining team of terrific people who need you to lead them forward!

So, feel the feelings and move on and up.

LAYOFFS, WORKFORCE REDUCTIONS, AND JOB ELIMINATIONS

> *"There are years that ask questions, and years that answer."*
> —*Zora Neale Hurston* [97]

In the spring of 2020, I found myself having to recite some version of the above to some of my team members who were subject to the sudden and searing job eliminations that our employer was in the process of conduct-

---

97   Zora Neale Hurston, Their Eyes Were Watching God (New York, NY: Armistad, 2006).

ing because of the economic shockwaves rippling through the globe during the COVID-19 pandemic.

At the same time, many departments went through a re-org as a result of these layoffs. Many manager-employee relationships changed in an instant as a sizeable portion of the team morphed into a new reporting structure. For my part, I was moved into a different role and inherited a different team that had been reduced in size by 50 percent, having just lost half of their coworkers because of a highly downsized revenue forecast for the year.

These decisions were made in a matter of days. We then had only hours in between when our CEO announced the job reductions and when managers had to deliver the news over Zoom, of course, because of the pandemic. I, like many of my coworkers, was overcome with nausea each time I learned the name of every individual who was impacted, many beloved teammates, solo providers for their families, and generally good-hearted people.

And this wasn't like a normal layoff. Rather, it was a sudden and jolting shred of head count in the middle of a global pandemic and uncertain economic situation. People were dealing with the trauma of the loss of their income in addition to homeschooling their children, not having the in-person support of their friends and family, and the general anxiety related to contracting COVID-19.

Of course, the work itself didn't go away overnight. Managers were in the position to re-allocate the work from the impacted employees, at times needing to make split-second decisions about who would be taking what type of newly orphaned projects, and then having to deliver that news to the remaining team on top of everything else. Woof.

The remaining team was in a state of shock, of course, but not surprised. It was a time in history where many companies were reacting similarly, making tough decisions to aggressively conserve cash. We all had a sense that it was coming, and the company communication back-channels had been pinging relentlessly with speculation. After the fact, many of the remaining team members reported a sense of almost having a survivor's guilt, grappling with some existential and practical questions like, Why was I spared?

It was...horrible.

Yes, layoffs do happen, and they are just plain awful. From a business perspective, it is often an unfortunate consequence of a Black Swan–type of event that requires the business to make hard decisions to aggressively conserve cash. It was probably one of the worst, if not the worst, days in my entire management career. Seeing people leave their jobs so abruptly, knowing many of them were primary breadwinners, and entering an uncertain period of time given the stress and unknowns of the pandemic and economic recession. Combining that stress with stepping up to the plate in taking the lead with a brand-new team who was rattled and shaken with the trauma of having lost so many of their beloved teammates was hard.

The business cycle is cyclical by definition. There are bear markets and bull markets, and the repetition of boom and bust times is likely inevitable. So, chances are good that at some point in your career, you will find yourself having to deal with a downsizing situation of some kind.

Layoffs are handled very differently from company to company, at least operationally (who does what and when), but it's likely you will be asked at some point to deliver some bad news personally to some people on your team. It might go something like this:

"I've called you into this meeting to inform you that, unfortunately, your position has been eliminated, and there is no other position for you at the company. That means you are being laid off. HR will work with you to complete your transition.

"I want to take this moment to thank you for your work over the years and say that I am very optimistic for your career in the future. You have an excellent work ethic, are a fast learner, and have a lot of great experience to offer.

"I know this probably feels like a shock and is pretty upsetting, so you don't have to say anything right now. HR will be working with you on your next steps as this transition occurs. I'll let you speak with them next."

If and when you are in a position to lead during a massive upheaval like this, know that this is the moment to really provide the absolute best leadership skills you've honed over the years. Empathy, creativity, tenacity, and grit will all serve you well during these times. It's easy to lead during boom times where success is rampant, but leading during bust cycles is much harder. This is where your leadership skills are desperately needed, and you have the greatest opportunity to make a difference and provide support. Do what you need to do to keep yourself sane and show up for your team to guide them through the challenge.

chapter 11

THE VITRUVIAN MAN(AGER)

"Time abides long enough for those who make use of it."
—Leonardo da Vinci[98]

The quintessential Renaissance man, Leonardo da Vinci, was fascinated by the intersection of science, humankind, and spirituality. In the 15th century, his sketch of the Vitruvian Man expressed this exploration of the human and the divine, conveying his belief that everything connects to everything else.

The Vitruvian Man depicts supposedly divine body proportions imagined by da Vinci.[99]

98 Maurice Walter Brockwell, Leonardo Da Vinci (Alexandria, Egypt: Library of Alexandria, 1908).
99 Takashi Ida, "'Vitruvian Man' by Leonardo da Vinci and the Golden Ratio," Advanced Ceramics Research Center, June 18, 2012, http://www.crl.nitech.ac.jp/~ida/education/VitruvianMan/.

Through the lens of history, we can suppose there are problematic aspects of this drawing: an ongoing affirmation of the patriarchy and maleness being a supposed divine way of being, the lack of inclusion of non-ideal body types, etc. Of course, we can and should view these historical artifacts with the appropriate criticism and our relatively modern context.

Nonetheless, there is something compelling about the exploration of the divine and the human and the constant striving to find meaning and purpose in our short lives. What does it all mean?

Today, we spend so much of the finite time we have in life at work. Our careers have become a prominent part of our lives, perhaps more than any other time in history. You have just moved into an entirely new phase of this journey, so where do you go from here?

Take another look at the Vitruvian Man.

Notice his arms moving up and across, representative of da Vinci's fascination with the human form being able to fit in both a perfect square and a perfect circle. [100]

Maybe the Vitruvian Man and we managers aren't as different as we seem, as pompous as that may sound.

In your new role, you will be reaching out upwards and to the sides, too. And while you may not be the perfect square or circle, your metaphorical

---

100 Kelly Richman-Abdou, "The Significance of Leonardo da Vinci S Famous "Vitruvian Man" Drawing," My Modern Met, August 5, 2018, https://mymodernmet. com/leonardo-da-vinci-vitruvian-man/.

touches to leaders at your side, as well as your own management chain, starting with your own manager, are important components to your coming into your own and rallying support around your company.

Let's start with your relationships with your new peers.

MANAGING ACROSS THE AISLE

"I have seen that in any great undertaking it is not enough for a man to depend simply upon himself."
—*Lone Man (Isna-la-wica)* [101]

Now that you're officially in your new upgraded manager role, take a good look at the updated org chart. Specifically, look to the left and then to the right and note all of the individuals who are now on the same level as you. Do you know these people? You need to.

To be an effective representative of your team, you have to really embrace that status when you're working across the aisle. No longer are you just simply representing yourself to these individuals who, just yesterday, were your superiors.

You're basically the new kid in town and have a lot to prove. But you already knew that.

Cross-departmental relationships are just as important as your relationships with your team, and are often overlooked by first-time managers since they don't initially seem as critical to invest in.

---

101 "We Are Part Fire, And Part Dream: Aboriginal Inspiration, in Aboriginal Voices," Indigenous Works, accessed May 19, 2021, https://indigenousworks.ca/en/resources/articles-reports/fire-and-dream.

This makes sense when you consider that your peer group would have been other individual contributors (IC) just a few weeks or months ago, so these new norms of communicating across other heads of departments as a status quo will take a while to percolate. The problem with this oversight is that you are essentially isolating your team by doing so and not building the credibility and rapport that you will need to be effective in working with other leaders in the company.

So, what will this feel like?

Well, it's uncomfortable at first. You have to establish yourself as a leader with this group who may, at first, be skeptical of a first-time manager. But, like it or not, you're going to have to prove yourself to them.

As an IC, your own manager probably invested at least some effort and time into facilitating your professional relationships across the org. As a manager, you can expect very little of this; you're a fully-fledged manager yourself now, and when it comes to navigating the minefield of peer relationships, you're kinda on your own!

Some examples of this might be facilitating a change in R&Rs (roles and responsibilities), escalating a cross-department deadline putting a project at risk in your department, and aligning on interdepartmental goals. You may need to develop OKRs (objectives and key results) alongside other leaders in your division, and you may need to divide up new work into buckets that each team tackles according to their strengths.

You'll also be expected to solicit performance feedback on your team members from other managers as well as provide this feedback for ICs in other departments. This is what I like to think of as managing across, and it's just as important as the more frequently cited concepts of managing up and managing down.

To give you an example, let's say you're the new head of sales. Look across at your peers: the heads of marketing, heads of product, and heads of customer support and customer success. Do you think you'll be successful running a sales department without working in lockstep with these other departments, in isolation?

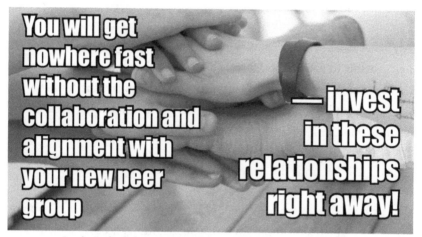

You will get nowhere fast without the collaboration and alignment with your new peer group —invest in these relationships right away!

Look to the left and then look to the right in the org chart.
These are your new homies.

The most frequent misstep I see when people attempt to manage across is to come in as a bull in a china shop, speaking in hotheaded hyperbole about what needs to happen in other departments in order to best enable your team. Coming back to the sales example:

"My team cannot close enough deals because the marketing team is terrible at generating enough leads to fill our pipeline goals. The whole team needs to go."

Hot tip: Don't be *that* guy.

But also, don't trend towards being deferential to other managers just because you're the noob:

"I think our team is having some trouble closing deals, but I'd defer to the marketing department to find a solution."

Ick! Don't do that either.

Somewhere in the middle:

"My team is frustrated that they're not finding enough valuable leads in their pipeline to meet their quotas. I'd love to collaborate with the marketing department to figure out how we can both populate the funnel a bit more as well as help our sales team be more effective at closing deals faster. What do you think, marketing team?"

Can you tell the subtle difference in these messages?

The last one is the most effective, because it clearly outlines that you are a true representative of the team that you're leading, accepts some of the responsibility for improving (coaching the team to close deals faster), and anchors the challenge to the process (building a sales funnel) and not the team. It also then professionally prompts the marketing team to respond in a collaborative way and sets them up to be the hero of solving this issue. Well done!

Managing across is a science and an art. You'll get better at it with time as you learn your own communication style, feel more confident in your role, and earn the respect of your colleagues. But keep this in mind—taking affirmative and assertive positions in cross-departmental matters on behalf of your team will deliver them the wins to build their loyalty and trust in you, represent them well on their behalf, and invest in the trust bank that is required to motivate them to excel.

MANAGING YOUR MANAGER

"If you don't ask, you don't get it."
—*Unknown*

As a new manager, it's critical to establish a functional, supportive, and affirming relationship with your own manager, who may or may not be someone new in your line of reporting based on your org chart.

This is obviously important for all the reasons it's always helpful to have a good relationship with your manager, no matter where you fit on the org chart: quality of life, personal growth, mentorship, feedback, etc. But now, there is the new element of having your entire team also be a stakeholder in you and your manager's ability to work together as a leadership team to elevate the entire department and help you grow into the badass leader your team needs to succeed.

So, it's time to manage up, buttercup!

When people refer to managing up, they generally mean exerting your management presence upwards or towards your own manager or management chain. Managing down refers to directly managing those who formally report to you in your organization. Your effectiveness in doing so will be increased by doing many similar things that are described throughout this book.

Relationships, communication, a deep knowledge of your business and space, and bringing your authentic self to these interactions are all critical to effectively managing your own manager. This is especially important as someone who is new and who will require a fair bit of coaching and support in your first few months out of the gate.

The reality in today's fast-paced world is that you probably won't have the luxury of hours and hours of loosely structured time with either your boss or your boss's boss, so it's important to be efficient and effective when interacting with your own management chain. Here are a few tips I recommend as a general approach to managing your manager:

1. **Come prepared, every time, with a light agenda and keep time.** This sends the message that both your and their time is valuable and you intend to use it well, and it builds confidence that you run a tight ship.

2. **Ask for introductions to your boss's connections** to help you network, unblock you or your team, or mentor you on a specific goal. Inevitably, your boss's inner circle will be at a higher level than yours, and this is a great way they can add value to your working relationship. It also shows them that you look up to their career and value their input.

3. **Ask them to meet one-on-one with any team member** you think might be struggling or isn't being challenged enough. Sometimes a skip-level meeting can work wonders in breaking through with a team member in need of a little extra support.

4. **Work with them to find opportunities for you** to present to other departments or even at an external industry meeting. This can really help you build your brand at the company, and your team members are counting on you to conduct yourself as a thought leader in order to give you their full trust.

Your first management role is also a terrific opportunity to get a ton of useful feedback from your own boss, who is probably very invested in your success, because if you fail, they have also failed by promoting someone who didn't do a great job. So, take advantage of that mutual interest and ask for lots of coaching. Sometimes you'll need to be specific and provide prompts, so here are a few to get you started:

- How would you rate my effectiveness at representing the needs of the team to other departments?

- Do you think I'm prioritizing the right things?

- How am I coming off to other leaders in the department?

- What are parts of the business or industry you think I should learn about to be a better manager?

- What do you perceive as my blind spots as a manager?

- Where are my natural strengths that you think I bring to the table?

Asking these questions with regularity can help you analyze your performance and know where to quickly focus on to meet the demands of the role and start good habits that will help you succeed at management and propel you forward to whatever is next in your career!

What if you're in a situation in which you're not having a great experience with your own manager?

Cue the world's saddest trombone noise.

I hate to say it, but this is a very common complaint I hear from first-time managers, especially millennials, probably because their leadership chain is experiencing a significant amount of burnout or has been a veteran of the industry so long that they may actually be a little out of touch with the realities of managing a team in today's uniquely challenging circumstances. I try to always give my own boss the benefit of the doubt and not overextend them when I sense they are having their own burnout. I think of us as a team, and that usually pays off when I need to really engage them or ask them something specific!

Or, let's face it—it could be because they're just not very good at their jobs. It happens. The world is filled with mediocre middle managers, and many of them are just not going to wow you or bring their A game to your relationship.

My advice: Let this mediocrity and disappointment motivate you as what not to do and find ways to make the relationship and time valuable for what it is.

Surely there's something this individual can contribute to your career and your team's growth—make it your personal challenge to take advantage of that. Dig deep if you have to. Does this person have a good network so maybe you can get introductions to other leaders in their industry? Do they have a specific technical skill that helped propel them to their success that you can absorb? Do they have a good perspective on a part of your industry that you can discuss and learn from?

If it is the worst-case scenario—and you really can't think of anything that is valuable from the relationship—you'll have to default to just learning from their mistakes and internalize what not to do in your own career. It's not going to be fun, but you'll simply have to push through it and make the most of a crappy situation for your team's sake.

In the long run, this reporting relationship won't last forever (even though it might feel like it) and probably won't last more than a year or two in today's economy where job roles and reporting relationships move fast.

Whatever you do, do not vent to your team or make it obvious in any way your relationship is strained. It's very important for the team to see a united front, and if necessary, explicitly discuss with your manager how important that is for your success.

It takes great professional maturity and emotional resilience to push through a period where you have a disappointing manager and still bring your A game each and every day, but trust in your ability to manage the challenge and use it as fuel to develop your own bad self into the leader you were born to be.

It's a very difficult situation to take on a management role where you don't have a great relationship with your own boss, but this will ultimately make you a better leader, so lean into the challenge!

REPLACING YOURSELF

In Lin-Manuel Miranda's smash-hit Broadway production of Hamilton, one of the most shiver-inducing songs involves then-president George Washington crooning his famous farewell address. In this legendary and renowned speech, Washington admits there is more he could do for the fledgling nation, but that his stepping down to ensure the peaceful transition of power was more important for the long-term stability than any other contributions he could have made.

Admittedly, with the hindsight of history, we have come to know the Founding Fathers' depiction in epics like Hamilton as problematic. We know that most of them owned slaves,[102] the original sin of America, and

---

102 Anthony Iaccarino, "The Founding Fathers and Slavery," Britannica, accessed May 19, 2021, https://www.britannica.com/topic/The-Founding-Fathers-and-Slavery-1269536.

therefore our heroization of them doesn't appropriately convey the pain and suffering caused by the ongoing legacy of slavery in our country.

That said, it remains historically remarkable that the American colonies not only overthrew a world power but established a government and legal document, the Constitution, that has lasted for centuries and survived a Civil War, two world wars, and multiple periods of civil unrest.

Unlike many fledgling countries in that era, the US was not built around a cult of personality. The early political leaders of the United States, despite their shortcomings, seemed to have some indication about the criticality of establishing a legacy of transfers of power and the symbolic passing of the torch to future generations.

What will your legacy be as a leader in your own right?

You've hired a great team, coached your individual team members to greatness, built strong relationships with your peers, represented your department well to other leaders, and developed key skills to level up your game.

You've given killer performance reviews, effectively and compassionately managed through tough employee feedback sessions, and inspired your team to rally around a visionary goal and give back to their communities.

If after your tenure in management you can say all the above—wow! Consider yourself to have absolutely achieved greatness in this chapter of your career.

But what is the ultimate legacy if not to have created more managers?

We'll end this book on the most important aspect of your tenure in your role, which is, quite frankly, a succession plan in which someone on your team will rise up and not only replace you, but will also do it even better than you did, because you have invested so heavily in their development, openly shared lessons learned, and encouraged your team to aspire to even greater heights than you do.

Likely, this will happen naturally and inevitably as your team grows to a certain size and outgrows the ratio of manager to IC number—7:1 or so, in my personal experience—that is typical of your industry and space. In this scenario, you either have the option to hire from the outside or, more likely, promote from within.

If you've done your job well, you'll likely have two to three potential candidates to choose from. That is to say, you've effectively invested enough time and energy in your team to have mutually discovered a natural inclination towards management for a small handful of people, and you've nurtured and coached those individuals to work towards that path. You've given them plenty of opportunities to take on responsibilities and leadership roles outside the boundaries of their stated jobs and have not only shared your wealth of knowledge on a specific technical skill, but also encouraged them to develop their own approach to problem solving.

You've taught them how and not just what.

And so, when the time comes, you will be replaced and maybe even outdone by your protégés!

If and when you reach the milestone of needing to scale yourself by hiring another layer of managers, it's always a good idea to at least conduct some interviews with outside candidates, as this helps you measure the current temperature of the labor market for the role you're hiring for. And you'll be making a super tough decision on which way to go, possibly the most important decision of your career yet.

The entire process of bringing in new managers is brutal, as you'll most likely navigate some major disappointment from your internal candidates if you do hire from the outside.

If you hire internally, the candidates you passed over will have a hard time digesting the news as well, but hopefully you've worked with them enough to ensure they are receiving regular feedback and career check-ins so that you can provide concrete reasons as to why you've selected your next manager and give them an outlet to express their disappointment.

Empathize, but don't dwell.

It's just part of the job that you'll be making some tough and unpleasant decisions. Don't let this overshadow the joy and excitement at having made a huge difference for the candidate you've selected.

The ultimate leaders create and inspire other leaders and empower the team in a way that their role becomes obsolete.

Your job now is to train up your management team and not just your own direct reports.

And just like that, you've taken a major leap up the influence and impact ladder. You've leveraged yourself up from the box of hiring the people who do the work to hiring the people who hire the people…

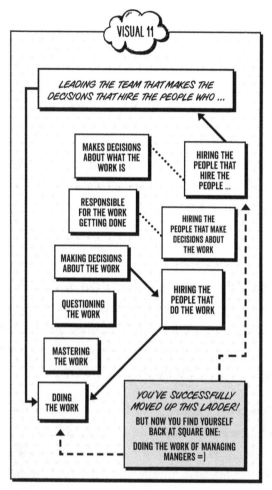

Congrats, you've upleveled! But now, you start all the way at the bottom again in your new role of a manager manager. Let's call it manager squared just for fun.

And yet, just like every quantum leap in your career level, you're also back at square one, doing the work. Just like when you started your first management career, you have a whole other responsibility and focus on developing your managers, navigating your new peer group, growing your own skill set by a certain percentage, and so forth.

So, what is actually next for you in terms of the career pyramid? Likely, you've upgraded your title and pay scale in one large go by hiring your new management team to report to you, so is the next step just to keep going up and up and up until you become CEO or something?

You could go a few different ways. Your situation is unlike any other, and certainly not one that can be effectively guided in a business book. That said, there are a handful of concrete possibilities that you should consider as you look to your next phase.

Considerations for your next move are as follows:

1. **Moving laterally, leading a similar team or function.** A solid next move is to take on responsibility for leading a team whose work you've done and come up in. A move like this, where you are shifting laterally into another manager role, is best done after you've achieved mastery or near-mastery of people-management basics.

2. **Moving laterally, leading an unfamiliar team or function.** This is going to be a real challenge, but taking on a leadership role in a department or function that you haven't done yourself is a good way to level up as a manager. Ideally, you'll have at least some adjacent or related experience that you can rely on to understand the basics, and you'll also bring at least one relevant skill that you can use to coach the team. At some point, if you keep moving upward within your industry or company, you're going to be taking on new teams that you haven't personally hired or come up from, so doing this early in your career can be a terrific move.

3. **Changing industries and starting over in an IC role.** You may reach a point in your career journey where you want to change industries or break into a space that interests you. Likely, you won't be qualified to go into a management role right away, but you could certainly build

back up into doing this later on. It's a perfectly good move to revert to a nonmanagement role to learn the tools of the trade, and don't worry too much if you end up taking a pay cut to do so. Your lifetime earnings will benefit from your having gained experience across multiple disciplines, so be strategic and go for it if you feel compelled to make a move!

4. **Deciding management isn't for you.** Be real with yourself. If you have come to the conclusion that having direct reporting relationships with your team is just not a good fit, or maybe you've moved into a chapter of your life where the responsibility is no longer appealing, you can move out of it into another role. You still have plenty of opportunity to be a leader and coach without the direct responsibility of management and can always explore this option again later as your circumstances and professional interests change.

5. **Continuing to move up in title and reporting responsibility.** This is the option that is the most obvious on the traditional career ladder. You go from manager to senior manager to director to senior director, etc. But be warned: Your foundational knowledge will be very specific, and you won't be developing a strong baseline skill set. If you do decide to pursue this direct upward movement, ensure you are challenging yourself with projects and ongoing learning about other facets of the business and building a network outside of your direct organization to be a more balanced leader.

You are the captain of your own ship, but no matter what you decide to do, remember to stay humble as you acknowledge your accumulation of power and influence. You are but one of an entire network of leaders navigating the modern world and putting their hearts into creating lasting change. People management is one of the most critical tools we have to transform the world to be a more equitable, prosperous, and joyful place for all of us.

And many people have not yet had the experience of having an incredible manager.

You are in a position to change lives, some in ways you will never know. Know your power and use it wisely to leave a legacy that will outlive you.

chapter 12

NOW WHAT? REPRISED

So, what will they say about us, the millennial managers stepping up to the plate, 50 years from now? What will future textbooks write about how the business community responded to the historic challenges such as systemic racism, widening inequality, and the climate crisis? What will they surmise about what went through our heads as we tried to make sense of the modern world?

On March 13, 2020, Breonna Taylor, a 26-year-old ER technician, was shot and killed in her bed by plainclothes officers in Louisville, Kentucky. The officers forced entry into her apartment as part of a botched investigation into drug-dealing operations. Breonna's boyfriend, Kenneth Walker, was inside the apartment with her and thought the officers were intruders, so he fired a warning shot at them.

The officers fired 32 shots in return, six of which lodged in Breonna's body as she slept, never to wake up again. [103]

---

103 "2 Officers Shot in Louisville Protests Over Breonna Taylor Charging Decision," the New York Times, updated April 16, 2021, https://www.nytimes.com/2020/09/23/us/breonna-taylor-decision-verdict.html.

Her home was never searched.

Breonna's story is one of many tragedies that fills our social media feeds. They serve as a horrific reminder of the thousands of Breonnas who exist— promising lives cut short not just at the hands of a police officer, but also by the chokehold of systemic oppression.

This is a challenging moment on an unprecedented scale. We know that racism lingers in all corners of the world, but the challenges don't stop there. Widening inequality threatens social stability on a massive scale. For example, only about 41 percent of Americans would be able to cover an unexpected $1,000 expense. [104] Climate change is the most ominous existential threat of all. As just one painful example of the danger of a warming planet, a third of Florida could be underwater by the end of the century. [105]

It's not enough to be outraged. Yes, outrage is an appropriate reaction, but it isn't enough. Outrage is a feeling, but without collective, sustained action, these tragedies will endure.

Hindsight is 20/20, and it's easy to think back to dark times in history, such as Nazi Germany, the Jim Crow South, the Khmer Rouge, or the Rwandan genocide, and ponder, How could anyone in their right mind have thought these things were okay?

But when you're in it, it's hard to see the injustice until it culminates in a tragedy such as Breonna Taylor's needless death.

So, what should we do?

---

104 Megan Leonhardt, "41% of Americans Would Be Able to Cover a $1,000 Emergency With Savings," CNBC, January 22, 2020, https://www.cnbc.com/2020/01/21/41-percent-of-americans-would-be-able-to-cover-1000-dollar-emergency-with-savings.html.
105 Richard Luscombe, "Will Florida Be Lost Forever to the Climate Crisis?" The Guardian, April 21, 2020, https://www.theguardian.com/environment/2020/apr/21/florida-climate-crisis-sea-level-habitat-loss.

Many, many business leaders have changed the world for the better and yet often for the worse. History has the final say. People like Andrew Carnegie, John D. Rockefeller, Warren Buffett, and Bill Gates have forever etched their names into our collective story about how and why the world is the way it is.

How do we remember them now? How did they use their power to serve humanity and advance the world? What societal challenges did they fail to identify and respond to in their respective time periods? What, if anything, is regrettable about their legacy?

Of course, this thought experiment isn't actually an experiment at all, because we only get one shot at this thing called life. There are no do-overs. As such, your career is not a dress rehearsal.

If you're reading this book, it's because you're determined to make the best of the opportunity in front of you. Consider yourself lucky. Only a small percentage of the population has the honor of leading human beings, and of those, a smaller percentage leverages their talents to deliver the kind of transformative leadership that changes the course of history, even on a local level.

You are going to be this kind of leader.

But you will make mistakes. You will have regrets. You will have bad days that feel like they never end.

Let these experiences shape your character. Let them develop your emotional resilience.

Wear your heart on your sleeve and fill your cup each day with the knowledge that you are an incredible human, capable of the deepest compassion and bravery to make bold decisions, inspire others to greatness, and as such have the capacity to write the next chapter of history a little better than before.

Feel it all. Let the experience touch your heart and teach you what you need to learn.

Thank you for letting me be a part of your journey.

GLOSSARY OF TERMS

360 Review – refers to a performance review that takes into account feedback from every reporting relationship relevant to the individual being reviewed. For example, feedback would be solicited from peers, direct reports, supervisors, and team members. These types of reviews are usually done once per year and are a lot of work, but they are super valuable because they ensure a representative selection of working relationships are included.

A/B Testing – involves a test of two different concepts to see which one directs users towards the desired behavior—e.g., do people click the Buy button more if it's blue or if it's purple? For a random half of the users, make it blue, while the other half sees purple. Which group clicks the button more?

ABR (Annual Business Review) – pretty much what it sounds like; is often used to describe an annual summit of sorts between customers and their vendors to review the previous year's performance and establish goals for the upcoming year.

API (Application Programming Interface) – sounds fancy, and it actually is fancy! This refers to a digital connection between two unique software systems that transmits information digitally between endpoints in the context of a business relationship. As a common example, do you use your Google or Facebook login to use another system or application? That's a use of the Google or Facebook login API to securely send your credentials between the two systems.

Agile – a style of project management characterized by grouping tasks into short periods of work, usually called sprints, and the frequent re-evaluation and evolution of plans based on lessons learned and feedback. The goal is to be a self-improving process and one that can change direction quickly if necessary.

ASAP (As Soon As Possible) – if you don't know this one, you may need a different book.

ARR (Annual Recurring Revenue) – super important financial/growth concept for tech companies. With SaaS companies, ARR is king. Or queen. Or whatever Harry and Meghan are now. Because SaaS companies aren't selling a thing so much as a service, revenue should be predictable, recurring, and scalable. Therefore, ARR basically shows how much revenue you expect to make based on these recurring subscriptions.

Backend – okay, I'll admit I used to blush every time I would hear this word because it sounds so, well, PG-13. But the real definition of the word is quite less saucy. It simply refers to the part of the software system or application that is not directly accessed by the user. The backend is usually for storing or using the data. You could also think of this as the infrastructure of a software system.

Bandwidth – in this context I am not referring to anything related to your personal Comcast internet hell. Actually, take that back. I am, in a way. Bandwidth in a business/workplace context refers to the general workload someone has and their capacity to absorb more projects or responsibilities. As a manager, you should refine your sense of what your individual team's bandwidth is when committing them to new projects.

Best of Breed – the best product of its type, for a particular use-case. Common example: An accounting software is almost never the best at being both an expense-tracking and a financial-accounting software. If you are responsible for buying both types of software for your company, you'll need to decide if you're going with a piecemeal Best of Breed solution or a fully integrated one.

Best in Class – a type of product that is the clear leader in a particular category, but not necessary the best overall. You could probably say that Microsoft is the best in class for a business solution when it comes to corporate intranets, but not the best overall when it comes to virtual meeting software (Microsoft Teams might actually make you break out in hives).

Best Practices – you've probably heard this term before, but that doesn't make it suck any less. Best practices is basically a gross-sounding corporate term for procedures, standards, and methods that are accepted as being correct and the most efficient. But before you feel like you want to barf by using this term, just accept that it's become corporate lingo that most people understand and does kind of make you sound smart. So, pop a Pepto and use it. That is to say, best practice is for you to use the term best practice. Capishe?

BOD (Board of Directors) – aka the suits. The concept of having a Board is pretty much ubiquitous in business and nonprofits alike, but their roles and responsibilities vary widely across industries and how companies are structured. For a public company, a BOD is typically an elected group of governing individuals that represents shareholders and sets certain operating policies, as well as the huge role of hiring executives. For all practical purposes, if you hear stirrings of "what the Board thinks" or "there's a new Board member" in your workplace, it's a big deal.

Buy-In – having someone's buy-in means you've convinced them of your way of thinking. It's a really important soft skill to be able to obtain buy-in from key leaders for any individuals or decisions you make, and your team will need to buy in to the direction you're leading them.

COB (Close of Business) – end of the workday, usually in the time zone of the person who is owed something, like an email response: "I received your email and will respond back by COB today."

Code Freeze – important to know if you work in anything tech (which is kiiinda all companies now). It's a point in time in the development process in which no additional changes can be added by software developers.

Content Marketing – content marking is cool. It's the creation and sharing of materials like videos, blogs, graphics, etc. that does not explicitly promote the brand, but it offers its own intrinsic value. The idea is that this type of content helps position the brand as a thought, which in and on its own will drive interest with potential buyers near the top of the funnel.

Churn – very bad. You don't want this. It measures how many customers cancel or do not renew their subscriptions with your firm.

C-Suites – a colloquial term for anyone with a job title that starts with a Capital C: CEO, CFO, CMO, and so on. Don't use this term in a super formal context, as it comes off as a little cheeky.

CTA (Call to Action) – generally a marketing term that specifies the very next step that you're trying to get the user to take. So, let's say you send out an email blast about your new product feature, and the CTA is that you want the user to sign up for a webinar to learn more about how to deploy said feature.

DAU (Daily Active Users) – an important metric in software. Refers to the total number of people who open and interact with your product in a given day. The DAU can offer insight as to users' behavior and can also be used as a measurement of growth of your product.

Deep Dive – not referring to swimming here; this is a very common business term for getting people together and conducting an in-depth analysis of a given topic.

Deliverable – yes, this word can be pretty much summed up by its etymology—that is, something is "able to be delivered." But it's actually much sexier than that and you should weave this into your work conversations to sound like a boss. Don't believe me? Say out loud: "I have a work project due on Friday" and then "I have a project deliverable on Friday." You're welcome.

Deploy – frequently used in tech to describe the push of a release to one or more machines or environments, thus updating the version that is considered current.

DevOps – sorry, but you're going to have to Google this one. I have been in tech for years and I still don't really understand WTF this is.

Disrupt – this is a fairly overused term in tech, but in my humble opinion it's still worth using. Disruption refers to a startup that is trying to break an existing industry rather than just improve on it. One could say, for example, that Uber disrupted the cab industry.

Ecosystem – in business this has a pretty similar meaning to the one from biology; it's more or less a network of companies that are all involved in the delivery of a product. Frequently used when describing a group of channel partners that integrate with a particular system.

EAP (Employee Assistance Program) – an outsourced counseling service provided by employers to assist employees who are experiencing personal challenges.

EE – employee.

EOD (End of Day) – distinct from COB; it could look a little sloppy if you promise something by EOD and it happens at 11pm.

ER – employee relations.

ERG (Employee Resource Group) – usually an HR-sanctioned special-interest group led by employees who self-organize based on interests or identities such as race or gender.

ESPP (Employee Stock Purchase Plan) – a common benefit of publicly traded companies, which offers employees the option to purchase company stock at a steep discount, and almost always benefits them financially. If your employer offers this, consider yourself lucky and encourage your team to learn more about it!

Equity – a general term for the portion of compensation for employees that is given in the form of some type of company ownership.

Fiscal Year – super important concept in sales and company finance; this measures the year-long period in which revenue and other metrics are measured. Often February 1 through January 31.

Frontend – similar to backend, it sounds saucy. And frankly, it kind of is. Frontend refers to the part of the software that is visible to users.

Gamify – common technique to encourage user adoption, to make it feel like you are playing a game. Some methods are to award badges, give points, or give competitive rankings to make using the software feel just a little bit more thrilling/addictive.

GTM (Go to Market) – describes the strategy and actionable steps that a company will utilize to bring their product to the consumers.

HTML (Hypertext Markup Language) – standard programming language for web pages. It's very useful to familiarize yourself with this a bit, as being able to make quick changes to web-based applications is quite handy.

IC (Individual Contributor) – someone who is not a people manager.

ISO (Incentive Stock Options) – allows employees the right to purchase stock at a discounted rate at a future date. The idea is that this fosters a sense of ownership in the employee as well as incentivizes them to do good work that increases the company value.

KPI (Key Performance Indicator) – a metric used to measure whether a business objective has been met. Might be something like, "At the end of this quarter, we will measure our success by having hired 10 new engineers."

Lean Six Sigma – project management method that focuses on elimination of waste through efficient team collaborations.

Learnings – an overly used, annoyingly sanitized term in the corporate world for a lesson learned. What this really means is "never fucking do that again." In the workplace, we call it a learning.

Metadata – commonly used term in tech that refers to the data about the data and is particularly useful when describing file transfers. For example, the metadata about the photos on your camera's photo roll includes the time, date, and GPS location where the photo was taken.

Move the Needle – corporate term for making a substantial impact.

MVP (Minimum Viable Product) – typically used in the software industry, MVP refers to the absolute basic functionality a product could have and still be useful. Common to use in agile methodology so feedback can be quickly gathered and incorporated into future iterations.

NPS (Net Promoter Score) – a score that is a widely-used measurement of customer satisfaction through a fairly simple calculation of the percentage of promoters minus the percentage of detractors. You've probably seen some product you use ask the question, "On a scale of one to 10, how likely are you to recommend product X to a friend?" Well, promoters are those who answer a nine or a 10, and detractors answer six or below. Passives are those who answer a seven or an eight.

Offsite – an offsite usually means that a team or department gathers in a location away from the office, away from distractions, and with a specific objective in mind, such as developing a product roadmap.

OKR (Objectives and Key Results) – in business this is a project management tool used by teams and by individual members to set goals, and then defined by what metric that result will measure.

Open the Kimono – don't ever say this. It's really gross sounding. But if you happen to hear it thrown around, it basically means to reveal important information.

Organic – not the expensive section of the produce aisle. In tech, this refers to the type of growth that happens naturally, like one of your users telling their friends about your company's product rather than your company spending money on advertising to target that same person.

OTE (Overall Total Earnings) – includes an employee's base pay in addition to the highest potential variable amount, such as an annual bonus or sales commission.

Out of Pocket – when someone is out of pocket, it means they are unreachable. "I'll be out of pocket starting Monday, so please let me know if you need my help on anything before then."

Point Solution – describes a collection of disparate software in which each addresses just one business need, rather than a more fluid, integrated enterprise approach.

Ping – a very overused term that is hard to describe. It's like a very informal communication intended to assess the status of something or simply to notify someone of a piece of information. Like a virtual poke? Honestly, I dislike the term ping, but it is a distinct type of workplace communication that justifies its own word.

PIP (Performance Improvement Plan) – a contract of sorts between an employee and the company (usually drafted by the manager—you!) that delineates specific areas of improvement and how they will be measured.

Pipeline – this term is used it many different contexts. In general, it describes a journey that a particular business process goes through to arrive at its desired outcome. For example, there could be a pipeline of talent for recruiting purposes, a pipeline of leads for sales purposes, or a pipeline of data for data management purposes.

Release – very important concept in tech. It describes the final version of a particular version of software being deployed to a production environment (the one where your customers use the software).

RSUs (Restricted Stock Units) – employee compensation in the form of company shares. They receive a market value when they vest and are then considered income. Normally a portion is withheld to pay the associated income taxes.

QBR (Quarterly Business Review) – a once-per-quarter meeting of a business unit, very common in sales organizations. It may also occur between a customer and the vendor to review metrics, set goals for the future, and discuss common interests.

R&Rs (Roles and Responsibilities) – not rest and relaxation. But done right, it can lead to that. In a business context, it's an agreement between departments or individuals that describes who is responsible for what and when.

RFI (Request for Information) – typically used in a sales context when a prospect issues a formal notice that they are gathering information for a prospective purchase. Can be a very lengthy document.

RFP (Request for Proposal) – once a prospect has reviewed an RFI and finds it agreeable, they may issue an RFP, which is a formal notice for a sales proposal.

SaaS (Software as a Service) – the future of software isn't on premise servers and CD drives—it's in the damn cloud! SaaS describes this type of product that performs a service for the buyer, and isn't an actual piece of software that is being sold.

Scalable – critical operating concept when a company is in growth mode. Does the thing you are doing become less expensive over time? For example, cooking a dinner for two people is less work than cooking two dinners. Cooking for groups scales nicely.

SEO (Search Engine Optimization) – a fancy marketing term for making your company's website more likely to come up in search results. It's a neat trick, and there's a lot of secrets to this that are on my very long to-do list to learn for my own website.

Silos – as a manager you'll likely hear complaints about people or teams working in silos. Yes, it's a reference to a grain silo. It just means that people are in their own little worlds, and not collaborating or coordinating with other teams. Easy to do in theory, but in practice it's actually hard to do.

SKO (Sales Kick Off) – an annual conference many companies hold to explain their sales strategy, present financial goals, and in general jazz up the troops about the upcoming year. These are often gaudy and boisterous affairs, but they are hella fun. Attendees usually have sales or sales-adjacent roles like marketing and are key leaders throughout the organization.

Soup to Nuts – old-timey way of saying an end-to-end solution, but surprisingly common in the business world.

Stack (or Tech Stack) – the set of technologies that a company uses to develop its framework. For a person, their tech stack is the programming languages they speak.

Stickiness – describes how your product tends to stick with your end users. Tricks like gamifying or providing a pleasing UI are common ways to make products stickier.

SWAT Team – in business this usually describes a cross-functional team of people who comes together to quickly address a major operational issue or deliver some kind of asset. It's a reference to the military on purpose; it's supposed to elicit a similar kind of adrenaline-like work ethic to pump out some deliverable really fast.

TC (Total Comp) – a measure of compensation that includes everything else, like bonuses, commissions, PTO, and contributions to medical insurance.

TCV (Total Contract Value) – very distinct from ARR but a good measure of the relative importance of a single deal. Measures how much total value a contract is worth, including the ARR and any one-time charges like installation fees.

Thought Leader – kind of the grown-up, white-collar version of an influencer.

UI (User Interface) – the graphical layout of an application. Might include the buttons a user pushes, text that they read, images, etc.

UX (User Experience) – more abstract than UI but even more important. Describes the journey and set of interactions the user has with the product, and the sense the user feels while interacting with the application.

Uplevel – used frequently in performance conversations amongst managers and HR-type folks, refers to the process that an individual goes through to achieve the next level in their career (not necessarily concurrent with a promotion). As they gain greater capabilities and more capacity for output and volume, we say they are upleveling.

Uptime – usually expressed as a percentage, uptime measures the time in which a product or service is functional and in operation (opposite of downtime).

Vesting Schedule – this refers to the schedule when assets that are promised to an employee fully vest, or become owned by the employee. For equity like RSUs, this is usually on a four-year schedule with a one-year cliff, meaning that nothing can vest in the first year.

War Room – like the SWAT reference, a War Room is supposed to elicit an urgent response to a serious challenge or work effort required to deliver some major project. Often required when a there is a very bad product, a seriously unhappy customer, or even an unexpected financial audit. May even be a literal room where people work hard over many hours!

Waterfall Method – project-management approach that is much more linear than agile. Requirements are gathered at the beginning of a project and then sequential milestones are derived, taking into account any critical pathways that produce the desired results.

Wire Frame – a skeletal model that displays a visual model for what a product will eventually do.